Christian Psalms
for Worship and Prayer

Christian Psalms
for Worship and Prayer

CHRISTOPHER L. WEBBER

RESOURCE *Publications* • Eugene, Oregon

CHRISTIAN PSALMS FOR WORSHIP AND PRAYER

Copyright © 2019 Christopher L. Webber. All rights reserved. Except for brief quotations in critical publications or reviews, no part of this book may be reproduced in any manner without prior written permission from the publisher. Write: Permissions, Wipf and Stock Publishers, 199 W. 8th Ave., Suite 3, Eugene, OR 97401.

Resource Publications
An Imprint of Wipf and Stock Publishers
199 W. 8th Ave., Suite 3
Eugene, OR 97401

www.wipfandstock.com

PAPERBACK ISBN: 978-1-5326-7886-8
HARDCOVER ISBN: 978-1-5326-7887-5
EBOOK ISBN: 978-1-5326-7888-2

Manufactured in the U.S.A.   06/05/24

Contents

Introduction: Gemstones and Veins of Gold   vii
List of Psalms   ix
The Psalms   1
Bibliography   273
Index of Authors   275
Thematic Index   287

Introduction

Gemstones and Veins of Gold

Between two and three thousand years ago, a number of songs were written that were so used and loved and valued that a collection of them was made for continuing use first in the synagogues of the Jews and then in the churches of the Christians. A contemporary Christian scholar, Bishop N.T. Wright, has called them "the daily life blood of Christians." Hymn books abound, but none can replace the psalms.

Not only do the psalms provide irreplaceable statements of faith and praise, they do it in a way uniquely adapted both to public worship and private prayer. The Hebrew psalms are poetry of a special kind, lacking the clear and definite rhythms of so many of the familiar Christian hymns, but with a unique rhythm of their own. Unlike the familiar hymns with their definite syllabic pattern and rhyming of sounds, the Hebrew psalms provide a looser structure and usually rhyme ideas rather than sounds. They are especially suited both to public recitation and to private meditation.

Yet the psalms can create problems for modern users. They come from an age unimaginably different from ours and take for granted patterns of life unfamiliar to most of us. Perhaps we can picture the world of the shepherd who leads a flock beside still waters (Psalm 23), but far more difficult to imagine is a world of violence that dashes an infant's head against the rocks (Psalm 132), or of sexual inequality that says to the princess, "The king is your master"(Psalm 45). There are psalms and portions of psalms that are never used in contemporary worship.

Meanwhile two thousand years of Christian life have produced eloquent expressions of faith that are seldom if ever used in worship. Most of the hymns we sing were written in the last two centuries. Earlier expressions of prayer and praise were written in other languages or in older forms of English and so are seldom used. But what if some of those expressions could be adapted to the rhythms of the Hebrew psalms and so made available both for responsive readings or psalmody on Sunday morning and for individual prayer and praise and meditation? What if even more modern expressions of prayer and praise could be adapted for those purposes?

It was with those questions in mind that I set out to quarry the mines of Christian faith where gemstones and veins of gold might be found. The resultant collection of psalm-like readings will never replace the ancient psalms, but perhaps they might provide useful alternatives for some occasions. In their present form they could be used in public worship wherever a psalm or responsive reading might otherwise be used. They could also be easily "pointed" for use with plainsong or Anglican chant and hymn writers might find them a source of inspiration for new hymns. Finally, the use of these texts may introduce contemporary Christians to some of their ancestors in the faith and lead them to explore further a wealth of resources often overlooked to strengthen our faith and expand our vocabulary of praise.

The texts are presented in a random order so that, like the Biblical psalms, they can be used consecutively with a constant change of mood and emphasis. The reader is not locked into a series of medieval psalms or a series of penitential psalms, but is constantly experiencing a variety of moods and styles of prayer. Indexes at the end provide guides to particular themes and authors that will be especially useful in planning public worship.

List of Psalms

Psalm	Source
1 What God Is Like Mine?	Anne Bradstreet (1612–1672)
2 Eternal and Gracious God	John Donne (1572–1631)
3 Mercy Must Be On My Mind	Richard Rolle (1290–1349)
4 Let It Be Your Joy to Serve God	Richard Rolle (1290–1349)
5 Consider the Dignity of Human Life	Nemesius of Emesa (4th Century)
6 God Has Showed Us	Julian of Norwich (1342–1416)
7 Before All Things, God Is Love	Simone Weil (1909–1943)
8 O Lord, Clothed with Majesty	Thomas Traherne (1636–1674)
9 Highest, Most Powerful	Francis of Assisi (1182–1226)
10 We Human Beings	John Donne (1772–1631)
11 The Whole of Creation	Julian of Norwich (1342–1416)
12 Let Us Sing	Saint Augustine of Hippo (354–430)
13 I Fled from God	Francis Thompson (1859–1907)
14 We Praise You, O God	T. S. Eliot (1888–1965)
15 We Never Rightly Enjoy The World	Thomas Traherne (1636–1674)

X LIST OF PSALMS

16	God Speaks to Those Who Serve	Julian of Norwich (1342–1416)
17	God Spoke to Me	Pierre Teilhard de Chardin (1881–1955)
18	Sometimes the Radiance of Love	Howard Thurman (1899–1981)
19	So I Saw That God Is Our Peace	Julian of Norwich (1342–1416)
20	The Angels of Heaven Have Joy	John Donne (1572–1631)
21	Do Not Be Strangers	John Donne (1572–1631)
22	I Long for God	Ingmar Berman (1918–2007)
23	There Is a Voice	Henri Nouwen (1932–1996)
24	Seeking Reconciliation and Peace	Brother Roger of Taizé (1915–2005)
25	God Comes to Those	Pierre Teilhard de Chardin (1881–1955)
26	God Created the World	Ladislaus Boros (1927–1981)
27	Our Earthly Life	Ladislaus Boros (1927–1981)
28	O Holy Fire	Hildegard of Bingen (1098–1179)
29	I Will Speak to My Lord	Thomas à Kempis (1380–1471)
30	Let Our Study Always Be	Thomas à Kempis (1380–1471)
31	Come, Lord Whom My Heart Desires	Symeon the New Theologian (c. 970–1040)
32	What a Wonderful Change	Walter Hilton (1340–1396)
33	A Clear and Pure Love	Catherine of Genoa (1447–1510)
34	Once Again I Have Fallen	Michel Quoist (1921–1997)
35	You Seized Me	Michel Quoist (1921–1997)

36 We Acknowledge, Lord God	M. Moran Weston (1910–2002)
37 The Greater Part of the Human Race	William Law (1686–1761)
38 Descend, Lord God	Daniel Payne Alexander (1811–1893)
39 Since, Lord, You Came	Michel Quoist (1921–1997)
40 Love for the Poor	Mother Teresa (1910–1997)
41 The Ways of Error	Soren Kierkegaard (1813–1855)
42 What Matters the Most	Brother Roger of Taizé (1915–2005)
43 I Heard a Voice from Heaven	Hildegard of Bingen (1098–1179)
44 True and Perfect Obedience	Meister Eckhart (c. 1260–c. 1327)
45 My Life Was in Turmoil	George Herbert (1593–1633)
46 In Years Gone By	Absalom Jones (1746–1818)
47 The Desire for God	The Cloud of Unknowing (14th Century)
48 The Glory of God	Dante Alighieri (1265–1321)
49 Listen Carefully to Instruction	Benedict of Nursia (480–547)
50 What Better Gift Could God Give	Bernard of Clairvaux (1090–1153)
51 Let Us Glorify Obedience	Phillips Brooks (1835–1893)
52 The Wandering Mind	Bernard of Clairvaux (1090–1153)
53 Grant Me, Lord God	Thomas Merton (1915–1968)
54 Love In Human Flesh	Edward N. West (1909–1990)
55 What Is It That We Seek	Dorothy Day (1897–1980)

xii LIST OF PSALMS

56 Paul May Plant	Maria Stewart (1803–1880)
57 Permit Me, O Lord	Elizabeth Rowe (1674–1737)
58 Lord, What Are We	Richard Crashaw (1613–1649)
59 Lead Me, Light of God	John Henry Newman (1801–1890)
60 Where Is the Secret Treasure	Jean Pierre de Caussade (1675–1751)
61 The Holy Spirit Leads Me Gently	Mechthild of Magdeburg (1207–c. 1290)
62 Deep Within Us	Thomas R. Kelly (1893–1941)
63 Let Us With Pure Hearts	Clement of Alexandria (150–215)
64 Beyond All Else	Alfred Noyes (1880–1958)
65 Strangely, You Come	Anna Bunston De Bary (1869–1954)
66 Pure Prayer Occurs	Wycliffite Spirituality (14th Century)
67 What I Ask For	Dag Hammarskjöld (1905–1961)
68 Like the Sun at Noonday	Dante Alighieri (1265–1321)
69 How Sweet a Thought	Richard Baxter (1615–1691)
70 Sun, Moon, and Stars	Alfred, Lord Tennyson (1809–1892)
71 Eternal Lord and Creator	Sophronius of Jerusalem (560–638)
72 You the Creator	William Barclay (1907–1978)
73 You Are Risen	Eric Milner-White (1884–1963)
74 Enter My Heart	Eric Milner-White (1884–1963)

75 I Do Not Need Any Hope	Simone Weil (1909–1943)
76 Thousands and Thousands of Years	Christopher Fry (1907–2005)
77 Truth Beyond All Truth	Lancelot Andrewes (1555–1626)
78 Consider the Treasure Within	William Law (1686–1761)
79 I Would Like to Be Free	Karl Rahner (1904–1984)
80 God Is Not Loved Without Reward	Bernard of Clairvaux (1090–1153)
81 You Promised, Lord	Bernard of Clairvaux (1090–1153)
82 How Can I Serve You	John Baillie (1886–1960)
83 Let Us Seek to Enlarge Our Souls	Lucretia Mott (1793–1880)
84 Now Let Us Sing the Eternal Life	Pseudo-Dionysius (5th to 6th Century)
85 Love Is More Precious Than Gold	John of Forde (1140–1214)
86 Christ Is the King of Glory	Martin Luther (1483–1546)
87 When I Searched for the Meaning	Hilary of Poitiers (315–367)
88 Weigh All My Faults	Christina Rossetti (1830–1894)
89 Peace Does Not Come from Terror	Oscar Romero (1917–1980)
90 I Was Felled to the Ground	Anonymous (c. 7th Century)
91 Eternal Joy and Blessing	Anonymous (14th Century)
92 You, Lord, Have Loved Me	Marguerite Porete (1250–1310)
93 Understand and Consider Aright	Jacob Boehme (1575–1624)
94 The Lord of Hosts Protects Us	Desiderius Erasmus (1466–1536)
95 I Have Seen a Mountain	Mechthild of Magdeburg (1207–c. 1290)
96 You Are the One	Geoffrey Studdert-Kennedy (1883–1929)

97 How Well I Know   John of the Cross (1542–1591)

98 Come Now, My Friends   Anselm of Canterbury (1033–1109)

99 God of Justice and Truth   Anselm of Canterbury (1033–1109)

100 I Saw a Tree in the Winter   Brother Lawrence of the Resurrection (1614–1691)

101 Where, Then, Am I Called to Go   John Bunyan (1628–1688)

102 Tell Me, O Human Heart   Hugh of St. Victor (1096–1141)

103 Listen to the Silence   Madeleine L'Engle (1918–2007)

104 How Fragmentary Is Human Existence   Ladislaus Boros (1927–1981)

105 All Glory Is Yours   Lancelot Andrewes (1555–1626)

106 The Only Way to Express Our Love   Dorothy Day (1897–1980)

107 O Love, Beyond All Knowing   John Baillie (1886–1960)

108 God Has Plans for a Future of Peace   Brother Roger of Taizé (1915–2005)

109 Blessed Are You, O Lord   Elisabeth Leseur (1866–1914)

110 If You Would Be a Servant of God   Abba Philemon (7th century)

111 Learn to Let Go of God   Anonymous (14th Century)

112 My Heart Has No Rest   Nicholas of Cusa (1401–1464)

113 Varied, Indeed, and Marvelous   John of Forde (1145–1214)

114 I Know That the Almighty God Is Present   Jeremy Taylor (1613–1667)

115 Peace Is the Highest Good   Desiderius Erasmus (1466–1536)

116 We Look For the World   Francis Thompson (1859–1907)

117 We Come to You This Morning	James Weldon Johnson (1871–1938)
118 By the Way of the Shepherds	Theodore Parker Ferris (1908–1972)
119 Use Me Then	Dwight L. Moody (1837–1899)
120 Thanks Be to You	Catherine of Siena (1347–1380)
121 I Praise, Adore, and Worship	Leslie Weatherhead (1893–1976)
122 The Land is So Beautiful	Oscar Romero (1917–1980)
123 Come, for the Fields Are White	Evelyn Underhill (1875–1941)
124 Who Is There Who Truly Loves	John Chrysostom (347–407)
125 Listen to My Voice	Columbanus (543–615)
126 Why Are the Changes	Boethius (475–524)
127 Look Down, O God,	Martin Luther (1483–1546)
128 God Sees Us	Martin Luther (1483–1546)
129 You, O God, Are from Everlasting	Miles Lowell Yates (1890–1956)
130 Lord, Increase My Faith	George Appleton (1902–1993)
131 Take, Lord, and Receive	Ignatius of Loyola (1491–1556)
132 We Are to Be Like a City	John Winthrop, Thomas Jefferson, Abraham Lincoln, Franklin D. Roosevelt, Martin Luther King, Jr.
133 When Your Church Awakens	William Barclay (1907–1978)
134 I Turn to You	Harriet Beecher Stowe (1811–1896)
135 Our God, My God	Desmond Tutu (1931–)

136 When I Wake to a New Day	Eric Milner-White (1884–1963)
137 Happy Is She Who Is Called	Clare of Assisi (1194–1253)
138 We Are Those Who	Myles Coverdale (1488–1568)
139 Place Your Good Spirit Within Me	Charles Wesley (1707–1788)
140 Let Our Lives Be a Song of Praise	Elisabeth Leseur (1866–1914)
141 Let Us Run to the Brooks of Water	Augustine of Hippo (354–430)
142 God is the Inheritance of the Saints	Jonathan Edwards (1703–1758)
143 Be My Will, Lord God	Douglas V. Steere (1901–1995)
144 Praise God for the Sweetness	Christopher Smart (1722–1771)
145 No, Lord, I Will Not Feast	Gerard Manley Hopkins (1844–1889)
146 I Took Up a Pearl	Ephrem the Syrian (306–373)
147 Those Who See the Light	Irenaeus (c. 130–c. 202)
148 All the Blessings God Grants	John Wesley (1703–1791)
149 Our Faith Is Not Founded on Empty Words	Hippolytus of Rome (c. 236)
150 I Rise to Live This Day	Saint Patrick (5th Century)

Psalm 1:
What God Is Like Mine?

Anne Bradstreet (1612–1672)

1. What God is like the God I serve? *
   What Savior is there like mine?

2. Let me never turn away from you, *
   for truly I belong to you.

3. My thankful mouth will speak your praise, *
   my tongue shall talk of you.

4. Rise up high, my heart, *
   because of what God has done for me.

5. Go, worldly people, to your foolishness, *
   and pagans to your gods;

6. Let them help you in adversity, *
   and bless your times of trial if they can.

7. My God is not like your gods; *
   you yourselves can judge.

8. I have found God's love: I know God's power; *
   God has been my strength and support.

9. God is not a human being who might lie to us, *
   nor one who goes back on a pledge.

10. God's word has been pledged from on high; *
    I know that I will live.

11. The One who died but now lives for ever, *
    is faithful from age to age.

12. God is the beginning and the end, and the Everlasting One; *
    God is the One who gives me life forever.

Psalm 2:
Eternal and Gracious God

John Donne (1572–1631)

1. Eternal and gracious God, *
    you hold back your gift of perfect joy and perfect glory.

2. Your gift will come to us when we see you and know you, *
    then we will possess your joy in an instant and forever.

3. Here in this world you give us a foretaste of that joy, *
    so we can understand in part that treasure that will last.

4. Nature reaches out her hand to us with corn and wine and oil, *
    you fill the clouds that pour down their rain and snow.

5. Industry reaches out her hand to us
    with the fruit of our labor and that of others, *
        but your hand guides our hands in all that they produce,
        and the increase is from you.

6. Friends reach out their hands to help us, *
    but your hand holds up the hands that support us.

7. Continue your goodness to us, O Lord, *
    and the gifts you give to us and to all the world.

8. Grant that when your Son comes again in glory, *
    he will find us ready to give an account of our stewardship.

9. Grant that time may be swallowed up in eternity, *
    and hope swallowed up in possession.

10. May all those you have called to your salvation, *
    become a perfect offering to you.

11. May you be pleased with the offering we bring, *
    and may we find our joy in you for ever.

Psalm 3:
Mercy Must Be On My Mind

Richard Rolle (1290–1349)

1. Mercy must be on my mind, *
    and mercy must always be praised.

2. Mercy is considerate and kind, *
    mercy delivers me from my troubles.

3. I have often been blind to mercy, *
    and wandered in the wrong way.

4. I must call on mercy to lead me, *
    and guide me to the end of my life.

5. Lead me, mercy, when life comes to an end, *
    deliver me, mercy, from the power of evil.

6. Mercy is as strong as steel, *
    when we seek for it in the right way.

7. Seek for mercy, you who desire it, *
    mercy will never fail those who seek it.

8. The vision of mercy brings healing and renewal, *
    mercy is always on my mind.

9. I am glad to honor mercy, *
    mercy seems sweet to me and good.

10. I find mercy always in my Creator, *
    who made us by the Wisdom of God.

11. God of all, my Ruler and my strength, *
    I ask you to be with me always.

12. Then I will sing of your mercy, *
    in thankfulness that has no end.

Psalm 4:
Let It Be Your Joy to Serve God

Richard Rolle (1290–1349)

1. Let it be your joy to serve God always; *
    see how the world's wealth slips away.

2. Try to understand and see how love lasts; *
    your cares will be resolved and your pain turned to pleasure.

3. Set your thoughts on Christ, abandoning anger and pride; *
    when you truly seek for him, all will be well.

4. Those who love the world turn day into night, *
    and are defeated in this life and lose the life to come.

5. Those whose love is false must always begin again; *
    they lose the land of light and find death deep within.

6. Lift your heart in adoration and say, *
    "Christ is my salvation."

7. Learn to love the One whose love is everlasting; *
    keep God's love in your thoughts,
    let the love of God be your song.

8. Keep the commandments and avoid sinful choices, *
    turn from the games others play to win the love of God.

9. Consider the humility and poverty of Jesus, *
    remember his suffering and the crown of thorns.

10. Let your heart be strong to abandon worldly priorities; *
    seek only the love of God
    so at last you may see God's face.

11. In time of temptation, pray that grace will strengthen you, *
    to give you stability and power to continue in the right path.

12. Say to God, "Lead me to your light, *
    Fill me with your joy,
    let my soul burn with your love."

Psalm 5:
Consider the Dignity of Human Life

Nemesius of Emesa (4th Century)

1. Consider the dignity and value of human life: *
    for our sake God entered into human life,
    that we might share the life of God.

2. Who can fully express the pre-eminence of human life? *
    Human beings cross the oceans and contemplate the heavens.

3. Human beings study the nature of the most distant stars, *
    and gather in a harvest from the land and the sea.

4. Human beings gain all kinds of knowledge, and skill in various arts, *
    they pursue scientific inquiries.

5. Human beings learn to communicate across vast spaces, *
    indeed, we are able to communicate also with God.

6. Human beings explore the nature of all created things, *
    and give orders to creation.

7. Let us not then put our nature to shame, *
    or show ourselves unworthy of such great gifts.

8. Let us not trade the enjoyment of eternity, *
    for material pleasures that cannot last.

Psalm 6:
God Has Showed Us

Julian of Norwich (1342–1416)

1. God has showed us that God is everything for us, *
   all that is good and strengthening in our need.

2. God is our clothing, who in love wraps us around, *
   and holds us close so as never to leave us.

3. I see that God is everything that is good; *
   this is my understanding of God.

4. Consider something as small as an acorn, *
   that lies in the palm of your hand.

5. This is all creation in God's sight, *
   and we may wonder how it can continue to exist.

6. It exists and continues to exists, because God loves it, *
   all things have existence because of the love of God.

7. It is God who creates, it is God who sustains, *
   and it is always God who loves.

8. Until I am fully united with God, *
   I have no true rest or true joy.

9. We seek rest here in this world where there is no rest, *
   and this is why we are never at ease.

10. We have no rest here because we have no knowledge of God, *
    God is almighty, all wise, and all good;
    and in God is our true rest.

11. God wills to be known, *
    and God wills that we rest in God.

12. Nothing lower than God is sufficient for us, *
    and this is why we never find rest,
    until we look beyond all created things.

13. God has shown us that it is God's joy and pleasure, *
    that we come to God simply, and plainly,
    and empty of everything else.

14. This is the understanding God has given me, *
    that God is enough for all my needs,
    and I may ask for nothing that is less.

15. If I ask for less than God, I will continue to wait; *
    only in God I have all.

16. The word of the goodness of God is lovely to hear, *
    for God's goodness fulfills all creation,
    and all God's works for ever.

Psalm 7:
Before All Things, God Is Love

Simone Weil (1909–1943)

1. Before all things, God is love; *
    all that we desire is fulfilled in God.

2. The impossible desires within us are evidence of our goal, *
    they are good for us when we no longer hope
    to accomplish them.

3. When we turn away from God, we give ourselves up to
    the law of gravity, *
    we think we can decide and choose,
    but we are only a stone that falls.

4. Wherever supernatural light is absent, *
    we are subject to the law of gravity.

5. We are like plants that are given only the choice *
    to be in or out of the light.

6. Joy and suffering are equally precious gifts, *
    both must be savored to the full.

7. Through joy, the beauty of the world penetrates our souls, *
    through suffering, it enters our bodies.

8. The transforming power of joy and of suffering are
   equally indispensable, *
   > when either one comes, we must open the center
   > of our selves to it as we open the door
   > to the messenger of love.

9. The infinity of space and time separate us from God; *
   > how shall we seek for God?
   > How shall we move toward heaven?

10. Our steps in this world are governed by the gravity
    that weighs us down, *
    > we are incapable of moving toward God by our own efforts.

11. God crosses the universe to come to us, *
    > over the infinity of space and time,
    > the infinite love of God comes to possess us.

12. We have the power to consent to God's coming or to refuse; *
    > if we consent to God's coming,
    > God plants a seed in our hearts.

13. The growth of God's seed within us can be painful, *
    > but the day comes when the seed grows by itself.

14. A day comes when the soul consents to love, *
    > then the soul must cross the universe to go to God's presence.

15. The love within us is an uncreated love, *
    > it is the love of God for God that passes through us
    > and draws us into God's presence.

16. Those whose souls remain ever turned toward God
    while the nail pierces it, *
    > > find themselves nailed to the very center of the universe.

Psalm 8:
O Lord, Clothed with Majesty

Thomas Traherne (1636–1674)

1. O Lord, clothed with majesty, *
    my desire is to praise you.

2. With all the holy angels, *
    I desire to give you glory.

3. With all the saints triumphant, *
    I seek to celebrate your love,

4. For the eternal brightness of your infinite bounty, *
    for the freedom of your love,

5. For the gifts you have poured out on us, *
    for the bodies you have given us,

6. For the tastes on my tongue and the feeling in my hands, *
    and all the senses that enrich my life;

7. But above all for the glory of speech, *
    by which I am able to praise you.

8. For all the beauty in heaven and earth, *
    the melody of sounds and the richness of color,

9. The light of history admitted by the ear, *
    and the light of heaven brought in by the eye,

10. For the skill of human hands, *
    and the ingenuity of human minds,

11. For the marvels and mysteries with which the world is filled, *
    for sculpture and painting, for writing and printing,

12. For all the skills you have encased, *
    in the red clay shaped into human life,

13. That you chose to form us out of dust, *
    and breath into our lungs the breath of life,

14. That you choose to raise up the poor, *
    and put down the rich and proud,

15. That you call us by name, *
    and come to us in word and sacrament.

16. For these and all your gifts, *
    I offer you my praises and my self.

Psalm 9:
Highest, Most Powerful

Francis of Assisi (1182–1226)

1. Highest, most powerful, Lord of all goodness, *
    all praise and honor and glory and blessing is yours.

2. To you alone all praise belongs, *
    no mortal lips are worthy to speak your Name.

3. All praise to you through our Brother the Sun, *
    day bringer, light giver, beautiful and radiant.

4. All praise to you through our Sister, the Moon, and all the stars, *
    precious and beautiful, you set them in the heavens.

5. All praise to you through our Brothers, the Wind and Air, *
    clouds and storms and weather that give us life.

6. All praise to you through our Sister Water, *
    useful and humble, precious and pure.

7. All praise to you through our Brother Fire, *
    cheerful and beautiful, powerful and strong.

8. All praise to you through our Mother the Earth, *
    providing our home and our nourishment,
    bring forth fruit and flowers, herbs and trees.

9. Be praised, good Lord, by those who forgive each other
for your sake, *
   by those who endure sickness and hardship,
   by those who endure in peace.

10. Be praised, good Lord, for Sister Death, *
    all must come at last to her embrace.

11. Woe to those who die in sin, *
    blessings to those who die while serving you.

12. All praise and blessing and thanksgiving be yours, *
    may all people serve you in humility and faithfulness.

Psalm 10:
We Human Beings

John Donne (1572–1631)

1. We human beings are not separate islands, *
    each of us alone in the sea;
2. We are members of Christ the Savior, *
    baptized into unity with others.
3. When a grain of sand is washed into the sea, *
    the continent itself becomes smaller.
4. When my home or my neighbor's home is washed away, *
    the community is made smaller.
5. Any individual death diminishes all of us, *
    because we share a common life.
6. Never send a messenger to ask for whom the bell tolls; *
    that bell tolls also for you.

Psalm 11:
The Whole of Creation

Julian of Norwich (1342–1416)

1. The whole of creation is like an acorn in the palm of God's hand; *
    it exists and will always exist only because God loves it.

2. We need to know how little the creation is, *
    to know and to love the Creator.

3. We lack security and comfort in our lives, *
    when we seek security in the creation and not the Creator.

4. God is almighty, all wise, and all good, *
    all true security is in God alone.

5. God wills us to know and to rest in God's love, *
    nothing beneath God can give us rest.

6. We must learn to set aside all created things, *
    there is no security in them.

7. God has shown us what great pleasure the Creator finds, *
    when one simple soul comes to God without pretense.

8. God, of your goodness, give yourself to me, *
    you are enough for me,
    I ask nothing that is less.

9. God's goodness includes all creation, *
    it surpasses all else that exists.

10. God is without beginning or end, *
    God keeps us in love, and all this is of God's goodness.

11. The goodness of God is the highest prayer, *
    it reaches our deepest needs.

12. God's goodness gives life to the soul, *
    it strengthens us in virtue.

13. God's goodness is near to us everywhere, *
    God's goodness is always quick to respond to our need.

14. God despises nothing that has been made, *
    and comes to those who are poorest and most in need.

Psalm 12:
Let Us Sing

Saint Augustine of Hippo (354–430)

1. Let us sing Alleluias here on earth *
    while we live in anxiety

2. So we may sing Alleluia one day in heaven *
    where anxieties come to an end.

3. How can we not feel anxious here *
    where temptations assail us on every side?

4. How can we feel secure *
    when we must daily confess our sins?

5. How can all be well with us *
    when we pray daily, "Deliver us from evil?"

6. Yet in the midst of temptations, let us give thanks, *
    and praise the God who delivers us from evil.

7. Human beings are always debtors *
    but God is always faithful.

8. Scripture does not promise deliverance from temptation,
    but God promises strength to endure.

9. What joy there is in the heavenly alleluias *
    sung in security, without fear of adversity.

10. Here we sing alleluias in anxiety, *
    there we will sing them in security.

11. Here we sing them as those destined to die, *
    there we will sing them as destined to live for ever.

12. Here we sing alleluias as wanderers, *
    there we will sing them as those who have come home.

13. Let us sing then to lighten our labors, *
    let us sing to shorten the journey,
    let us sing till at last we come home.

Psalm 13:
I Fled from God

Francis Thompson (1859–1907)

1. I fled from God down many nights and days, *
    down through the arches of the years I fled.

2. I fled God down the winding ways of my own mind, *
    and hid in times of laughter and of tears.

3. I fled from God in times of gloom and times of fear, *
    I fled those feet that always followed me.

4. They followed with deliberate pace, *
    deliberate speed, majestic instancy, unhurried,
    constant, following.

5. I feared the One who might insist, *
    My love alone is all you ever need.

6. But fear is less able to evade, *
    than love is able to pursue.

7. I fled across the borders of the world, *
    and even looked up to the stars to seek escape.

8. I pleaded with the darkness to come, *
    but then I begged for the dawn.

9. I clung to the whistling mane of every wind, *
    but fear was less wise to evade, than love was to pursue.

10. Still with unhurried pace, deliberate speed, *
    those following feet came on.

11. A Voice insisted, "Nothing shelters you, *
    who will not shelter me."

12. I called on nature to conceal me, *
    and nature united me with herself.

13. I knew the face of the sky, *
    I knew how the clouds were formed;

14. My moods were united with nature; *
    I died each evening and came to life each morning;

15. I rejoiced in the sunlight, *
    and I wept in the rain.

16. But nature could not nourish me, *
    or ease my heart's ache,
    nor could we converse together.

17. Still the feet that followed me, *
    came on and ever closer.

18. With all deliberate speed, and steady pace, *
    those feet came after me,

19. And a Voice came faster still to say, *
    "Nothing makes you content,
    when you stay far from Me."

20. I stand defenseless now against Love's sword, *
    all my armor has been struck off;

21. I am driven to my knees, *
    and I cannot defend myself.

22. My days have gone up in smoke,
    and my years have turned to dust.

23. Even my dreams have come to an end,
    and my fantasies have been destroyed.

24. Must grim death and the grave swallow me up, *
    for the harvest of God to be gathered?

25. But now the long pursuit is ended, *
    and the Voice bursts upon me like the sea:

26. "All things flee from you, *
    when you still flee from me.

27. "You are so strange and pitiful, *
    so futile in your search.

28. "Human love must always be earned, *
    and what love can you have earned?

29. "Who will you find to love you, *
    save God, save only God.

30. "All that I took away from you, I took *
    so that you would come to me to find it.

31. "All that you considered lost *
    is stored up for you at home."

32. The footsteps halt beside me. Is my gloom *
    only the shadow of God's outstretched hand?

33. The Voice says, "Rise, now; take my hand; *
    rise, take my hand and come.

34. Oh, weak, blind, foolish one; *
    I am the one you seek."

Psalm 14:
We Praise You, O God

T. S. Eliot (1888–1965)

1. We praise you, O God, for your glory, *
    your glory displayed in all creation.

2. We praise you for the rain and the wind, *
    for the storms and the quiet days.

3. All things exist because of you, *
    they exist only in your light.

4. Your glory is made known even when it is denied, *
    the darkness declares the glory of your light.

5. All things affirm you in living: *
    the bird in the air and the beast on the earth affirm you.

6. Humankind also affirms you by living, *
    and praises you by thinking and doing.

7. The back bent in toil and the knee bent in prayer praise you, *
    the head bowed in grief and the hands raised in thankfulness
    praise you.

8. Forgive us, Lord, for shutting ourselves in, *
    for separating ourselves from you and from each other.

9. Forgive us our trespasses and our weaknesses, *
    forgive us for violence against others,
    and our lack of response to their needs.

10. Forgive us for fearing human injustice, *
    and being forgetful of your perfect justice.

11. Lord Jesus, by your suffering and death, *
    have mercy upon us.

Psalm 15:
We Never Rightly Enjoy The World

Thomas Traherne (1636–1674)

1. We never rightly enjoy the world, *
     till we value it more than any treasure.

2. Can we take too much joy in the world God made? *
     God is in all that world.

3. The glory of all things is spiritual, *
     and understood by the mind, not the eye.

4. We never rightly enjoy the world, *
     till we see the glory and wisdom of God
     revealed in a grain of sand.

5. Water and wine may quench my thirst, *
     whether I think about them or not.

6. But to see that they flow from the love of God, *
     quenches the thirst of angels.

7. To take pleasure in all their benefits, *
     is to live in the life of God.

8. We never rightly enjoy the world, *
     till we awake every morning in heaven;

9. Till we see ourselves in the Creator's world, *
     and look on earth and air and sky
     as gifts of the love of God.

10. The bride and groom who stand at the altar,
    have less reason for joy *
        than those who see God in Creation.

11. We never rightly enjoy the world, *
        until the sea itself flows in our veins,

12. Until we are clothed with the heavens, *
        and crowned with the stars,

13. And we see ourselves truly to be, *
        the sole heirs of all the world,

14. And we understand that everyone else, *
        is sole heir of the world as well.

15. Until we can sing and rejoice and take delight in God, *
        as misers do with gold and kings with scepters,
        we do not enjoy the world.

16. Until our spirit fills the whole world, *
        and the stars become our jewels,

17. Until we love others and seek their happiness, *
        with a thirst as great as for our own,

18. Until we take delight in God's goodness to all, *
        we never enjoy the world.

Psalm 16:
God Speaks to Those Who Serve

Julian of Norwich (1342–1416)

1. God speaks to those who serve, *
    saying, "Take these words and believe them;

2. "Hold fast to these words; *
    trust in them and find strength;

3. "This is the promise made to God's people: *
    You shall not be overcome.

4. "These words shall vanquish all evil: *
    You shall not be overcome."

5. Belief in these words is comfort and strength, *
    to all the people of God.

6. These words bring confidence and courage, *
    whatever troubles may come.

7. God does not promise that we will not be troubled,
   that we will have no distress, *
    but we shall not be overcome.

8. It is God's will that we trust in these words, *
    that we trust in good times and bad,

9. God loves us and seeks us, *
    and God wills that we love God also.

10. God wills that we love and trust God, *
    and we shall not be overcome.

Psalm 17:
God Spoke to Me

Pierre Teilhard de Chardin (1881–1955)

1. God spoke to me and said, *
    "You called me and I am here.

2. "You had need of me in order to grow, *
    and I am waiting for you to make you holy.

3. "You have always desired me, without knowing it, *
    and I am always at work
    drawing you to myself.

4. "I am the fire that consumes, *
    and the water that overflows.

5. "I am the love that begins, *
    and the truth that passes away.

6. "I am all that compels acceptance, *
    and I am all that brings renewal.

7. "I am the one who breaks apart, *
    and I am the one who binds together."

8. The world beloved of God has a soul to be redeemed; *
    receive the spirit of the earth to be saved.

9. In heaven all things are one, *
    in heaven all things are one.

Psalm 18:
Sometimes the Radiance of Love

Howard Thurman (1899-1981)

1. Sometimes the radiance of love is so gentle and soft *
    that all harsh lines seem to be wiped away.

2. Sometimes love's strength seems to surround us *
    and weakness is nowhere to be found.

3. But sometimes the radiance of love *
    kindles fires grown cold from despair,

4. And sometimes new fires are kindled *
    by a hope without beginning or end.

5. Sometimes the radiance of love *
    blesses life with a vision of new possibilities

6. And sometimes love calls forth self-judgment *
    and strikes us with hopelessness and despair.

7. Sometimes love shows us forgotten weaknesses *
    and bears witness to our unworthiness.

8. But love has no awareness of merit or demerit; *
    love has no scale to measure or weigh its portion.

9. Love never seeks to balance giving and receiving. *
    Love simply loves; that is its nature.

10. But love is not blind, or naive, *
    and love is never false or pretentious.

11. Love holds us securely in its grasp, *
    calling everything by its true name.

12. Love surrounds all things with its wisdom; *
    it avoids mere sentimentality.

13. Love enables the true self to come to life, *
    and love makes all things new.

14. The experience of love outlasts all things, *
    but love is never diminished or lost.

15. No created thing can be the source of such fullness
    and completeness. *
    God alone can hold us
    with a strength so far beyond our own.

16. No circumstance, no condition, no hardship outside ourselves *
    can separate us finally from the love of God
    nor from the love of each other;

17. And so we pour out our gratitude, *
    giving thanks to God that this is so!

Psalm 19:
So I Saw That God Is Our Peace

Julian of Norwich (1342–1416)

1. So I saw that God is our peace, *
    and keeps us safe when we lack peace
    and works constantly to bring us into peace.

2. And our Lord keeps us when we feel forsaken, *
    when we feel cast away because of our sinfulness.

3. The humility that we gain in this way, *
    with great contrition and true longing for God,

4. Raises us up by God's grace, *
    and brings us great joy with the saints.

5. By contrition we are made clean, *
    and by compassion we are made ready,

6. And by true longing for God, *
    we are prepared to come into God's presence.

7. And though we may be punished here with sorrow and grief, *
    yet shall we be rewarded hereafter by the great love
    of our Lord God,

8. For it is God's will that those who come to eternal life, *
    not lose the work that they have done,

9. And so shall shame be turned into worship, *
    and sorrow into great joy.

10. God wills that we should never despair, *
    for our failures never separate us from God's love.

11. We are not always in peace and love, *
    but peace and love are always at work in us.

12. God wills that we understand, *
    that God is the ground of our life in love,

13. And God is our everlasting keeper, *
    and defends us against all adversity.

Psalm 20:
The Angels of Heaven Have Joy

John Donne (1572–1631)

1. The angels of heaven have joy in your conversion, *
    and can you be without that joy in yourself?

2. Howling is the noise of hell, *
    singing is the voice of heaven.

3. Sadness is the depression of hell, *
    rejoicing is the serenity of heaven.

4. Those who lack that joy here, *
    lack the best evidence for the joys of heaven.

5. True joy in this world shall flow into the joy of heaven, *
    as a river flows into the sea.

6. This joy shall not be put out in death, *
    and a new joy kindled in me in heaven.

7. We need not wait for the possession of heaven,
   or the perfection of the sight of God, *
    until we have ascended through air and fire and moon.

8. Without the thousandth part of a minute's stop
   we shall come immediately to the glorious light of heaven, *
    for all the way to heaven is heaven.

9. The angels that come from heaven bring heaven with them
   and are in heaven here, *
    and that soul that goes to heaven meets heaven here.

10. As the angels do not put off heaven by coming to us, *
    so the departed put on heaven in going there.

11. We do not go to heaven because we lack joy here, *
    but so that our joy might be full.

12. As Christ promised that no one shall take our joy from us, *
    so neither shall death itself take it away.

13. In the face of death when it lays hold on me, *
    I shall see the face of God.

14. In the agonies of death and the sorrows of that departure, *
    I shall put on a more glorious garment above
    and be joy superinvested in glory.

Psalm 21:
Do Not Be Strangers

John Donne (1572–1631)

1. Do not be strangers to the face of Christ, *
    see him here that you may know him there.

2. See him in the sacrament of his word, *
    see him in the sacrament of the altar.

3. Look him in the face as he lay in the manger, *
    and do not murmur about your needs.

4. Look him in the face in the temple disputing with the doctors, *
    and apply yourself to meditation and conversation with God.

5. Look him in the face in his father's house as a carpenter; *
    take a calling and fulfill yourself in that calling.

6. Come closer and look him in the face on Good Friday, *
    when he who gives breath to all gave up his spirit.

7. Look him in the face again on Easter day, *
    raised victoriously in the destruction of death.

8. Look him in the face in his humiliation and exaltation, *
    that as you keep your eye on God, God's eye will be on you.

Psalm 22:
I Long for God

Ingmar Bergman (1918–2007)

1. I long for God but my heart is empty; *
    the emptiness is a mirror turned toward my own face;
    I am filled with fear and disgust.

2. I have no concern for others; I have isolated myself; *
    I live in a world of phantoms.

3. I am imprisoned in my dreams; *
    yet I seek to live and to understand.

4. Is it too much to ask that we know God here and now? *
    That we know with our human senses the one who created us?

5. Why does God hide from us in the mists of distant promises? *
    Why are the miracles always so far away?

6. How can we have faith in those who believe
when we have no faith in ourselves? *
    What will become of us who aren't able to believe
    even though we want to?

7. Why can't I kill the God within me? *
    Why does God live on though I curse him
    and try to tear him out of my heart?

8. Why in spite of everything is God a baffling reality *
    a shadow that clings to me wherever I go?

PSALM 22: I LONG FOR GOD

9. I seek for knowledge; not faith but knowledge; *
    I want God to reveal himself and speak to me.

10. I call out to God in the darkness, *
    but no one seems to be there.

11. If no one is there, life is an outrageous horror; *
    who can live in the face of death, knowing
    that all is nothingness?

12. Someday we must all stand at the last moment of life, *
    we must look toward the darkness.

13. In our fear, we make an image, *
    we fashion an image and call it our God.

14. Meanwhile life is a futile pursuit, *
    life is a wandering and talk without meaning.

15. Faith is a torment, a reaching out in the darkness, *
    a love for someone who never appears or answers.

16. Let me use my life for a meaningful deed; *
    let me fight against death while life remains.

Psalm 23:
There Is a Voice

Henri Nouwen (1932–1996)

1. There is a voice at the center of my life *
    that calls to me by name:

2. The voice says, "You are mine, *
    I have called you; you belong to me.

3. Before the universe came into being, *
    I knew you and called you by name.

4. Wherever you go, I am with you, *
    I keep watch over you day by day.

5. I have food to satisfy your hunger *
    and water to quench your thirst."

Psalm 24:
Seeking Reconciliation and Peace

Brother Roger of Taizé (1915–2005)

1. Seeking reconciliation and peace *
   requires struggling to find those gifts within ourselves.

2. The spirit of unity is not easily found; *
   the gift that endures must be paid for.

3. The heart must become more open; *
   it must overcome suspicion and be always kind.

4. We must walk the road of trust *
   and constantly renewed mercy.

5. Although we may often fail in our search, *
   we will learn that peace and communion are the gift of God.

6. Although we become discouraged, *
   we will learn to call down God's Spirit to heal our weakness.

7. Throughout our life it is the Holy Spirit again and again *
   that enables us to continue the search

8. And move from one beginning to another *
   toward the future of peace.

Psalm 25:
God Comes to Those

Pierre Teilhard de Chardin (1881–1955)

1. God comes to those *
    who offer themselves to serve.

2. The more our desires are centered on God, *
    the more God floods into our deepest self;

3. Where human beings love one another, *
    God is the bond of that love.

4. Christ binds us together, *
    and reveals us to one another.

5. What my lips fail to convey to another, *
    he will tell them better than I.

6. What my heart desires for them, *
    he will grant them if it is good.

7. Those who would be saved *
    must dare to love another more than self.

8. Salvation is bought at the price *
    of a risk incurred and accepted.

9. We must stake earth against heaven, *
    give up the security of the self-centered life,
    and risk everything on God.

Psalm 26:
God Created the World

Ladislaus Boros (1927–1981)

1. God created the world in hope *
    and set mankind in the world to fulfill that hope.

2. All creation bears God's life within it; *
    we have no existence apart from the Creator.

3. We were created to work with God, *
    to fulfill God's purpose in creation.

4. Hope and a taste for happiness *
    are vital to human life.

5. The Christian lives in history *
    with confidence in God's purpose.

6. Where life exists and a flame of love *
    we can see already what heaven is like.

7. The world comes to its fulfillment in Christ *
    who calls us to everlasting joy.

8. To be faithful is to live in hope *
    and to bear witness to the promise of life.

Psalm 27:
Our Earthly Life

Ladislaus Boros (1927–1981)

1. Our earthly life is far from God's reality; *
    we constantly pass God by.

2. We are dominated by people, things, and events, *
    controlled by our longings and dreams.

3. All these fill the horizon
    and hold us in their grip; *
    they leave no room for God.

4. But when there is nothing left, *
    God alone remains.

5. We must give up all that we cling to, *
    all possessions, and dreams and achievements,

6. For all these, though good in themselves, *
    are not God and keep us from our Creator.

7. We live in the world to transform the world *
    in hope of the glory to come.

Psalm 28:
O Holy Fire

Hildegard of Bingen (1098–1179)

1. O Holy Fire that brings peace to my spirit, *
    O fire of the spirit giving life to Creation;

2. You are a healing oil for the injuries that come to us, *
    healing for all our divisions and conflict;

3. O breath of holiness, O fire of loving, *
    O joy that fills the human heart
    and strengthens us to serve you;

4. O fountain of purity, pouring forth healing waters, *
    water of baptism, water of life;

5. O robe of life and hope for the faithful, *
    caring for all those in conflict and stress,

6. Break down the chains and restraints that oppress us, *
    help us set out on the path we should follow.

7. O way of holiness in the midst of confusion, *
    always in front of us wherever we may be,

8. In the high places and in the plains, *
    you call us and unite us;

9. You set the clouds in the heavens
 and the trees on the hillsides, *
   you set the streams on their courses
   and send rain in dry seasons.

10. You give us understanding so we may know your faithfulness; *
   you lift us up to rejoice in your goodness.

11. Praise be to you for the joy of life, *
   for hope and strength and light in our darkness.

12. Praise be to you, *
   O Spirit of God.

Psalm 29:
I Will Speak to My Lord

Thomas à Kempis (1380–1471)

1. I will speak to my Lord, *
    although I am only dust and ashes.

2. If I value myself above what I am, *
    my failures bear witness against me,
    I cannot deny it.

3. But if I acknowledge what I am, *
    you are merciful to me
    and bring light to my heart.

4. You make known to my heart what I am, *
    for I am nothing except through your gift.

5. Left to myself, I am nothing and weakness, *
    but when you come to me I am made strong
    and filled with new joy.

6. Weighed down though I am with trouble, *
    you embrace me and lift me up.

7. You go before me in my journey *
    and guide me in the midst of dangers.

8. In my failures I had lost you and my own self as well, *
    in seeking you I found myself also.

9. Your infinite goodness surrounds me day by day, *
   you seek even those who have turned away from you.

10. Transform me, faithful Savior, that I may make known your love, *
    you alone are my strength, my help, my life.

Psalm 30:
Let Our Study Always Be

Thomas à Kempis (1380–1471)

1. Let our study always be, *
   the life of Jesus Christ.

2. Those who follow his life and teachings *
   will never walk in darkness.

3. The teaching of Jesus surpasses that of all others; *
   those who have the spirit of Christ
   will find the hidden manna.

4. It is not good words that make a person holy *
   but a holy life that makes one dear to God.

5. If one were to know all the words of the Bible, *
   what use would it be without love?

6. Everything the world contains *
   is useless without love.

7. It is useless also to seek honor and position *
   without the love of God.

8. It is useless to seek riches and trust in them *
   and to lack the love of God.

9. It is useless to seek for length of days *
   and not a life given to God's service.

10. It is useless to be concerned for this life alone *
     and not for the life to come.

11. It is useless to love the things that are perishing *
     and to have no concern for the things that will last.

12. Those who follow their own desires *
     will lose the grace of God.

Psalm 31:
Come, Lord Whom My Heart Desires

Symeon the New Theologian (c. 970–1040)

1. Come, Lord whom my heart desires; *
    Come, my breath and my life.

2. Come to me, my joy and my glory; *
    Come to me, my love and my delight.

3. I give you thanks that you have become for me
        my day without an evening; *
    you are the sun who never sets.

4. You fill the world with your glory; *
    you never hide yourself from anyone.

5. You who are far removed in glory, *
    take me up in your arms.

6. The One who is here and shines in my heart *
    gives life to me, unworthy though I am.

7. I am given a share in the light, *
    a share in the glory of God.

8. I take my fill of the love and beauty of God, *
    who strengthens me and lifts me up.

9. Let no one distract my mind, *
    or turn my eyes away from looking toward the Light.

10. I see the Light that is truly Light; *
    I see the Source of all beauty,
    I see the Cause of all things.

11. I see the Beginning who has no beginning, *
    the Wisdom beyond understanding.

12. Again the light blazes forth to reveal God's love; *
    again the Light drives away all darkness.

13. The One above the heavens,
    whom no human being can see, *
        comes to live in my heart.

Psalm 32:
What a Wonderful Change

Walter Hilton (1340–1396)

1. What a wonderful change it is *
    to be known as a child of God.

2. To have all earth's treasure
   and command of all the world *
    would be a wonderful thing indeed,

3. And though it cost the love of God for ever, *
    there are many who would gladly have it;

4. But yet more wonderful, delightful beyond comparison, *
    the glorious changing of our lives toward God,

5. For there is a greater distance to go
   from the lives we live to the life of God *
    and therefore this turning is more wonderful than any other.

6. This turning toward God comes about in this life; *
    and this turning is a gift of grace.

7. Those who humble themselves and seek no worldly honor *
    must covet only the love of God;

8. They must be willing to be scorned by others *
    and treated as utterly foolish.

9. They must seek only to hold God in their hearts *
    and to see God there and devote themselves to God.

10. Often they will find that the God they seek *
    is present already within.

11. Then they will try to do nothing else *
    except to please and worship God.

12. This is a gracious change *
    beyond all price and value.

13. If then this change is so good, *
    why are we so slow to come?

14. Should we not seek constantly to accomplish it, *
    and study daily how to fulfill it?

15. Not wearily, heavily, dully, and unwillingly, *
    but with all the strength of the heart and a burning zeal,

16. For there is nothing so worthwhile and valuable, *
    nothing that can bring us such joy.

17. As often as we fall short, we must turn again *
    and ask God to forgive us and take us back.

18. No one can come to God *
    who is deeply bound to any other creature.

19. In God alone will we find what we long for; *
    in the love of God there is perfect peace.

Psalm 33:
A Clear and Pure Love

Catherine of Genoa (1447–1510)

1. A clear and pure love asks nothing of God *
    and is satisfied with none of God's gifts, however great,

2. A clear and pure love of God *
    seeks only for God.

3. Therefore I want no created love, *
    no love that can be grasped and tasted and enjoyed;

4. I want no love that comes through my understanding, *
    nor a love that comes through my will,

5. For a pure love transcends all these *
    and passes beyond them and says,

6. "I will not be content until I am enclosed in that place *
    where all created things lose themselves and are divine."

7. I have resolved to say to the world, *
    "Do with me outwardly what you will,
    but inwardly leave me alone,

8. "I have no wish or desire to center myself *
    elsewhere than only in God."

9. A clear and pure love is never content *
    to participate in God as other creatures do,
    some more and some less;

10. A clear and pure love seeks no comparison *
    but only to be in God.

11. So I find my being in God, *
    my strength, my joy, my happiness.

12. I find in myself by the grace of God *
    a love without fear of falling away.

13. To be plunged and submerged in the love of God *
    is like being submerged in the sea;

14. There is nothing but water on all sides, *
    nothing but the fire of love on all sides.

15. God came into our humanity *
    to raise us to the divine;

16. I seek to come to that place *
    where God's purpose is fulfilled in me.

Psalm 34:
Once Again I Have Fallen

Michel Quoist (1921–1997)

1. Once again, Lord, I have fallen; *
    how can I carry on?

2. I knew you were watching me, *
    and yet I fell.

3. Instead of looking toward you for help, *
    I turned my eyes away.

4. You watched in sorrow, *
    and let me go.

5. And now I find myself alone, *
    alone and ashamed of my failure.

6. My sins take possession of my life, *
    they hold me and will not let me go.

7. They flow in my veins, *
    they bring darkness into my heart.

8. You have loved me, Lord, and I have forgotten you; *
    I thought only of myself.

9. Your love weighs me down *
    with a weight beyond my strength.

10. I have no more strength; *
    I dare not make promises.

11. I lie at your feet, *
    forgive me and help me to rise.

12. Show me once again, Lord God, *
    your cross, my only hope.

13. Turn my heart toward your cross, *
    turn my face toward your light.

Psalm 35:
You Seized Me

Michel Quoist (1921–1997)

1. You seized me, Lord, and I could not resist; *
    I ran for a long time, but could not escape.

2. You followed me wherever I went; *
    I went off the main road, but you were there.

3. At last you overtook me *
    and I could run no longer.

4. You swept my doubts away, *
    and overcame all my fears.

5. And now, Lord, your presence is my life; *
    I look up and meet your gaze;
    I speak and I know that you hear.

6. You draw me closer as the moon draws the tides; *
    the fire of your love burns in my heart.

7. And now I have found the peace that I longed for, *
    the false light of the world fades away.

8. What once I desired and sought for *
    seems now to be worthless.

9. Nothing else matters except to be in your presence; *
    I want nothing except your love.

10. You have taken hold of my life, *
    you are my confidence and my only joy.

Psalm 36:
We Acknowledge, Lord God

M. Moran Weston (1910–2002)

1. We acknowledge, Lord God, that we do not see clearly, *
    nor fully understand what we see.

2. We acknowledge that we have too often been unwilling *
    to stand against abuses of power in church and state.

3. We acknowledge that we have often failed *
    to stand for the things we believe in.

4. Grant us, Lord God, the courage to hold our ground, *
    to make no compromise with evil.

5. Too often, Lord God, we have been content to conform, *
    satisfied to live as others do
    rather than live for others.

6. We acknowledge that we have too often failed to become involved, *
    we have been content to let others work for us.

7. We have lacked confidence, Lord God, in your power, *
    and failed to allow you to work through us for your will.

8. Renew us, Lord God; send your Holy Spirit to empower us; *
    enable us to be among those
    who bring light and life to your world.

Psalm 37:
The Greater Part of the Human Race

William Law (1686–1761)

1. The greater part of the human race seem to be asleep, *
    their thoughts and actions are like a dream;

2. The rich and the poor, the wise and the ignorant,
   are all in the same state, *
    they pass their lives away in a slumber.

3. For every man and woman has an eternity within, *
    and is born for eternal life.

4. And therefore those who do not have their hearts and minds
   set on eternity, *
    are like those who are fast asleep.

5. A life devoted to the interests and enjoyments of this world,
   spent and wasted on earthly desires, *
    has all the shortness and delusion of a dream.

6. Eternal life is as near to us now as this world is to our bodies; *
    we are created and redeemed to share that life forever.

7. God is not an absent or a distant God, *
    but is more present to us than our own bodies.

8. We are strangers to heaven
   and without God in this world *
    because we lack the Spirit of prayer.

9. Prayer alone can unite us with the one true God *
    and open heaven and the kingdom of God within us.

10. A root set in the finest soil and blessed with abundant rain and sun *
    is not as certain to thrive as the one whose spirit
    is turned to prayer.

Psalm 38:
Descend, Lord God

Daniel Payne Alexander (1811–1893)

1. Descend, Lord God, descend, *
    and let your glory fill this place.

2. Descend, and show us your mercy, *
    descend, and let your laws be made known.

3. Let your love cover us and spread abroad; *
    descend on us with your richest blessings.

4. Let the light of your holy truth dispel our darkness, *
    let your peace fill every heart.

5. Let the blind see and the deaf hear, *
    and let every mouth speak your praise.

6. When your people raise their voices in praise, *
    let their songs and hymns come before you.

7. When your children raise their voices in prayer, *
    hear us and come and make your presence known.

8. Let your justice strike fear among the oppressors, *
    let the oppressed shout for joy at your coming.

9. Let messengers go forth from this place with good news, *
    and let those who hear come to you in joy.

10. Come quickly, Lord God of our ancestors, come, *
    shine forth in splendor in this place.

Psalm 39:
Since, Lord, You Came

Michel Quoist (1921–1997)

1. Since, Lord, you came into my life *
    your light has searched me through and through.

2. Every day without mercy, *
    you show me the weight of my sins.

3. The light you shine on me, *
    shows me more than I can bear to see.

4. You show me all the obstacles *
    I place in your way;

5. I see my helplessness, *
    my inability to serve you as I should.

6. I see that all I can offer *
    is flawed because of my selfishness.

7. I see the depth of my failure *
    in the blinding light of your love.

8. Your light is merciless, Lord; *
    it shows me my weakness and failure.

9. Yet you, Lord, are merciful: *
    I have no hope apart from your mercy.

10. I give you thanks for the light that shows me my need; *
    I thank you for the light that shows me your mercy.

Psalm 40:
Love for the Poor

Mother Teresa (1910–1997)

1. Love for the poor is like a living flame: *
    in them we find the presence of the Lord.

2. Do not search for God in distant lands, *
    God is close to you; God is with you.

3. There are many people unloved and uncared for, *
    Christ is in them, but where are we?

4. Whatever we offer another:
    a smile or a piece of bread, *
    Jesus accepts as an offering to him.

5. There must be no pride or vanity in what we offer; *
    the work is God's work,
    if it is done in God's Name.

6. God thinks through our minds, *
    and God works through our hands.

7. We are all-powerful, *
    through God's strength in our lives.

8. Each act is only a drop in the ocean, *
    but the ocean is composed of drops.

9. Each individual matters to God, *
    Christ is present in each one.

10. Make us worthy, good Lord, to serve you; *
    give us strength to love you.

11. Help us to serve all those
    who live and die in poverty and hunger, *
       give them their daily bread through us;

12. Give them this day their daily bread, *
    give them peace and joy through us.

Psalm 41:
The Ways of Error

Soren Kierkegaard (1813–1855)

1. The ways of error are many, *
    but the Way of Truth is one.

2. There is One who is the Way and the Truth, *
    through whom we are led to Life.

3. Thousands upon thousands bear the Name *
    that proclaims their choice of a Guide.

4. They call themselves Believers, *
    they are pilgrims and strangers,
    and foreigners in this world.

5. To believe means exactly this: *
    that what I seek is somewhere else,
    that I am now on a journey.

6. To be faithful is to be restless, *
    to find no ease in this world.

7. The pilgrim is one with a goal, *
    who chooses a path to follow.

8. The pilgrim is one with a goal, *
    who chooses a Guide for the journey.

9. The pilgrim is one with a Guide, *
    who has gone the same way
    and met the same trials.

10. When we meet the same trials, *
    we can be sure we are following the same path.

11. When we walk the same path, *
    help is nearest when the need is greatest.

12. The joy of the journey is great, *
    when we follow the well-worn path.

13. There is only one way to follow, *
    in time and eternity one choice to make.

14. In life there is only one joy, *
    and that is to follow Christ.

15. In death there is one final joy: *
    to follow Christ into Life.

Psalm 42:
What Matters the Most

Brother Roger of Taizé (1915–2005)

1. What matters the most is the discovery,
   that God always comes to you *
      and that God loves you.

2. Even to those who think there is no God,
   even to those who think God doesn't love them: *
      God is always present.

3. Christ is always waiting, *
      to be welcomed by each person.

4. If you are unable to respond, *
      God will respect your silence.

5. But when at last you respond, *
      God is already present within.

6. If you have doubts and uncertainties, *
      these may be openings of faith.

7. Your faith does not create God, *
      and your doubts do not drive God away.

8. The simple desire for God, *
      is the place where faith begins.

9. Would you then let yourself fall asleep, *
      indifferent to God's presence?

10. Will you let yourself remain asleep, *
    believing you can make no difference
    and God is unable to act?

11. Or will you remain awake, *
    and be prepared to act?

12. Faith enables us to act, *
    to be agents of reconciliation.

13. Lord, let your light shine in my life, *
    help me to overcome the darkness
    in my life and the lives of others.

14. Your light, O Lord, shines within me; *
    let my heart welcome your love;
    let my heart share your love with others.

Psalm 43:
I Heard a Voice from Heaven

Hildegard of Bingen (1098–1179)

1. I heard a voice from heaven saying, "Write; *
    make known the splendor of the things you saw.

2. "Tell others how you saw a fiery light, *
    a light inflaming all your life with love."

3. I did not see these things in sleep or dreams; *
    I saw them with my inner eyes and ears.

4. I heard a voice from heaven saying, *
    "I am the Light; I illumine the darkness."

5. These visions did not come by human invention, *
    but by the secret mysteries of God
    I heard and received them in the heavenly places.

6. I heard a voice from heaven, saying, *
    "Cry out and write what you have heard and seen."

7. I saw a great mountain and enthroned upon it, *
    One of such glory that it blinded my sight.

8. The One upon the throne cried out, *
    "O fragile human, dust and ashes,
    cry out salvation's story.

9. "Unlock the mysteries that are too often concealed; *
    let the abundance of mystical knowledge burst forth.

10. "Arise, cry out, and tell what is shown to you *
    by the One who rules all creatures,
    who floods those who fear God with love,

11. "Who leads those who persevere in the way of justice, *
    to the joy of the Everlasting Vision.

12. "Where the Fear of the Lord leads, *
    those who are poor in spirit follow.

13. "The Fear of the Lord holds fast in humble devotion
    to the blessedness of poverty of spirit, *
        which seeks no boasting or pride of heart,
        but loves simplicity and sober minds."

14. Whoever does strong works of salvation, *
    obtains the upwelling fountain of glory.

14. Whoever has knowledge in the Spirit and wings of faith, *
    let them embrace the vision and receive it in their souls.

Psalm 44:
True and Perfect Obedience

Meister Eckhart (c. 1260–c. 1327)

1. True and perfect obedience to God *
    is a virtue above all others

2. No great work can be accomplished without it, *
    and all will be done better with obedience.

3. Obedience brings out the best in all things, *
    it never fails or goes wrong.

4. If you act in true obedience, *
    it will not fail to be good.

5. Obedience has no cares, *
    and never lacks a blessing.

6. When we have no will of our own, *
    God comes to us in due season.

7. When I give up my own will, *
    God must will for me.

8. When I deny myself, *
    God's will for me is identical with God's own purpose.

9. The best prayer we can offer is not,
    "give me virtue or give me life," *
        but only, "Lord, give me only what you will."

10. When we have achieved this prayer, *
    then we have prayed well.

Psalm 45:
My Life Was in Turmoil

George Herbert (1593–1633)

1. My life was in turmoil; I cried out, "O God!" *
    But God was in my grief
    and governed it for my good.

2. If God was not present in my grief, *
    I could scarcely have survived.

3. Your Spirit gives me life and hope, *
    your Spirit prays within me.

4. Your life on earth was filled with suffering, *
    and you continue to suffer in me.

5. Those who seek to avoid suffering, *
    seek to avoid sharing Christ's life.

6. Broken though I am, Lord, leave me here; *
    leave me between this world and the next.

7. My thoughts are like knives that give me no peace; *
    there is no way to avoid them,
    yet they wound my soul.

8. Nothing in all the world seems to give me life; *
    all the elements are against me.

9. Help me, Lord God; *
    scatter the darkness in me,
    as the sun scatters the night's darkness.

10. Then all those forces that work against me shall serve you, *
    and day by day work for my renewal.

11. With care and courage, they will build me up, *
    until at last I shall come into your presence.

Psalm 46:
In Years Gone By

Absalom Jones (1746–1818)

1. In years gone by, God saw with an eye of pity the affliction of our countrymen, *
    saw the wars stirred up to gain captives to sell as slaves.

2. God saw the ships fitted out from ports in Europe and America, *
    saw them freighted with trinkets to be exchanged for the bodies and souls of men.

3. God saw the anguish which took place, *
    when parent and children were torn apart.

4. God saw them thrust into the holds of the ships, *
    where many perished from the want of air.

5. God saw them exposed for sale, like horses and cattle, *
    like bales of goods, in warehouses and ports.

6. God saw the pangs of separation between members of the same family, *
    saw them driven into the sugar, rice, and tobacco fields.

7. God saw them labor beneath a burning sun, *
    saw them faint beneath the pressure of their labors.

8. God saw them return to their smoky huts in the evening, *
    with nothing but roots to satisfy their hunger.

9. God saw all the different modes of torture used on their bodies, *
   the whip, the screw, the pincers, and the red hot iron.

10. God heard the prayers that went up from the hearts
   of God's people; *
   and God came down to deliver them.

11. God came down into the United States Congress, *
   when the slave trade was ended.

12. God acted at last in bloodshed and tears, *
   to bring an end to slavery itself.

13. This land shall no more be stained with the blood of its children, *
   nor witness the anguish of families,
   parted for ever by a public sale.

14. For these great acts of the God of mercies, *
   let us this day offer up our united thanks.

15. Let the song of angels be heard in our assembly: *
   for these first fruits of peace upon earth.

16. Let us give thanks to the Lord: *
   let us call upon the name of the Lord,
   let us make known God's deeds among the people.

17. We thank you, Lord God, that you are no respecter of persons, *
   and that you have made of one blood all nations and people.

18. We give thanks that you came in the fulness of time, *
   in behalf of this nation and all its people.

19. We thank you that the sun of righteousness *
   has shed its morning beams upon us.

20. Rend your heavens, O Lord, *
   and come down upon the earth;

21. Grant that those mountains which obstruct
   the perfect day of your goodness and mercy towards us, *
   may flow down at your presence.

22. Hasten the time when the knowledge of the gospel
    shall cover the earth, *
        when the wolf shall dwell with the lamb,
        and the leopard shall lie down with the kid,
        and a little child shall lead them;

23. When instead of the thorn shall come up the fir tree, *
        and, instead of the brier shall come up the myrtle tree:

24. And it shall be to the Lord for a glorious name, *
        and for an everlasting sign that shall not be cut off.

Psalm 47:
The Desire for God

The Cloud of Unknowing (14th Century)

1. The desire for God is more pleasing to God *
    than the vision of all the angels and saints in heaven.

2. The blind stirring of love for God is better to have *
    than hearing all the mirth and melody of the saints in bliss.

3. Therefore let God draw your love upward *
    and strive through God's grace to forget all other things.

4. Those who seek God perfectly will not rest *
    in the remembrance of any angel or saint in heaven.

5. All that is not God, however good in itself, *
    prevents more than it profits
    the one who seeks God perfectly.

6. Let nothing else work in your wits or will, *
    but only the grace and the goodness of God.

7. The one who gains a true knowledge of self, *
    will soon come to a true knowledge of God.

8. Give yourself entirely to gaining a true knowledge of your self, *
    and that will be true humility.

9. Love and humility are God's greatest gift, *
    and those who have them need nothing more.

10. In beholding the love of God all nature quakes, *
    and all angels and saints are blind.

11. Love alone is perfect, *
    for love has no end.

Psalm 48:
The Glory of God

Dante Alighieri (1265–1321)

1. The glory of God who moves all things *
    penetrates the universe.

2. The splendor of God burns brightly, *
    but seldom is it seen
    and few are able to describe it.

3. Grant me, O gracious God, ability to speak *
    and sing that realm beyond our knowing.

4. All things bear the imprint of God's hand, *
    and all things are drawn to their Creator.

5. The sacred fire that lights all nature, *
    glows most brightly in those created in God's image.

5. Although the creature that is free to will *
    may stray from its course,

6. Sin alone is able to turn us from our way *
    and veil the image of God.

6. Yet as surely as streams run down to the sea, *
    so does the human spirit turn at last toward its source.

7. No human eye can endure the light *
    that blazes forth from the throne of God,

8. But that light shines out to us in human love, *
    and in the faces of those whose lives are turned toward God,

9. And only the light of truth *
    can give rest to our restless seeking.

10. Bible and church are provided for our salvation; *
    let us then be satisfied with the gifts we are given.

11. Let us follow steadily on the path before us, *
    and not be blown off course with every wind of controversy.

12. No seed does well on rocks or crowded by weeds, *
    so we must build on the foundation we are given.

13. Those who have once heard the heavenly chorus, *
    will be haunted till death by the desire to hear it again.

14. Look up then to the dwelling place of God *
    and seek the face whose gaze is fixed on us.

15. Seek for the fire beyond all human knowing *
    and that joy that lasts beyond all thought of time.

16. Just as the beauty of the rising dawn *
    exceeds in glory the rays of the western sun,

17. So must we come at last to a radiance beyond all knowing *
    and beyond all that human words can express.

18. There is the mind so dazzled and amazed *
    that awe and wonder kindle into flame.

19. There all our will and desire are moved by that love *
    that moves the sun and all the other stars.

Psalm 49:
Listen Carefully to Instruction

Benedict of Nursia (480–547)

1. Listen carefully to instruction *
    and meditate on it in your heart.

2. Obedience will bring you back to the God you seek, *
    from whom we drift away through lack of effort.

3. This message is for the one prepared to abandon self-will *
    and serve the true Lord in faithfulness.

4. Let us open our eyes to the light that comes from God; *
    let us listen to the Voice that summons us daily.

5. God waits for us daily to turn our faith into action; *
    God is patient, but now is the time to act.

6. Let us pray God to renew our strength and commitment; *
    what we do now has eternal value.

7. Let us not fear when the road is narrow; *
    patience and faithfulness will bring us great joy.

8. Let none of us seek our own desires, *
    but always the good of others.

Psalm 50:
What Better Gift Could God Give

Bernard of Clairvaux (1090–1153)

1. What better gift could God give us
    than the gift of God's own love?

2. The love of God is the truest love *
    since God's love seeks only to give.

3. Who else provides food for all who hunger *
    and air for all who breath,
    and light for every eye?

4. Who does not know that all our bodily needs *
    are provided by the Creator?

5. Who does not know that all human dignity *
    is the gift of the Creator?

6. Who does not understand that the gift of reason *
    comes from the Word by whom the world was made?

7. Who does not recognize that the sense of justice *
    calls out to love God with all our strength
    since all we possess is the gift of God?

8. Who is not ashamed to offer God so little *
    when God has given us so much?

9. Yet the more surely we know ourselves to be loved, *
    the easier it is to love in return.

10.   I cannot love as I ought, *
          but only as God loves me.

Psalm 51:
Let Us Glorify Obedience

Phillips Brooks (1835–1893)

1. Let us glorify obedience, *
    it is not slavery but self-control.

2. The one who obeys nothing, receives nothing; *
    to obey a living thing is to share its life.

3. Come to the experts and do as they say, *
    and all the wisdom and treasure they have acquired
    will then be open to you.

4. When God says, Do this and live, *
    that is not a bargain but the truth.

5. To disobedience the door is closed; *
    whatever wealth there may be is beyond our reach;

6. Obedience means self-mastery and possession, *
    therefore let us glorify obedience.

7. Obedience is life and light; *
    disobedience is darkness and death.

8. What folly it is to be selfish; *
    to say, I will spin my own music;
    I will not be obedient.

9. The wheel unbelts itself from the vast machine, *
    it whirls wildly into space,
    then drops to the sand and dies.

10. That is what some call life, *
    it is not life but dissipation.

11. Knowledge and will are strong, *
    but obedience is stronger.

12. Lord, grant me grace to come to you in obedience, *
    and by constant obedience to you
    to share constantly in your life.

Psalm 52:
The Wandering Mind

Bernard of Clairvaux (1090–1153)

1. The wandering mind rushes about *
    and seeks but is not satisfied.

2. These are the ones who constantly seek for more *
    and never enjoy what they have.

3. These are the ones who wander always in circles *
    wanting what they do not have
    and rejecting the means of gaining it.

4. They wear themselves out with pointless effort *
    and never come to fulfillment.

5. The desire to possess all things is a winding road, *
    a circle that repeats itself endlessly.

6. The just are not like that; *
    they choose the royal road,
    the road that leads to salvation.

7. They do not seek to possess all they see, *
    but to sell their possessions and give to the poor.

8. Money cannot diminish the mind's hunger; *
    more than air is needed to satisfy the body.

9. God stirs us to seek for love; *
    God sustains and fulfills.

10. God causes us to desire, *
       and God alone satisfies that desire.

Psalm 53:
Grant me, Lord God

Thomas Merton (1915–1968)

1. Grant me, Lord God, the gift of silence *
    to seek you and find you in quietness.

2. Teach me humility and obedience *
    to attend to your presence and your desires.

3. Teach me to think of you and not the world, *
    to desire to please you and not seek the world's satisfactions.

4. Teach me to trust you *
    and place myself more and more in your hands.

5. Teach me to know your presence with me in my work, *
    and to live and work in your company throughout the day.

6. Teach me to recognize your presence within, *
    and to taste the joy and peace of being with you.

7. When I am blinded by your light *
    help me still to trust.

8. When I cannot see my way *
    help me to wait in patience for your guidance.

9. When I am in suffering and darkness *
    show me signs of your presence.

10. When I am filled with a sense of affliction and defeat *
    let me not be drawn away from you
    by the world's attractions and rewards.

11. Grant me in times of darkness *
    to know your presence, living God.

12. Surround me, sustain me, *
    and in the darkness be my light.

13. Draw me always toward that deeper unity with you *
    in which all love and joy is found.

Psalm 54:
Love in Human Flesh

Edward N. West (1909–1990)

1. Christ is love in human flesh, *
    and love is God's only work.

2. Love is the grace God gives to the humble *
    who seek to live in Christ.

3. Love means re-birth; *
    becoming a new person in Christ.

4. Love means the glad completion of one's self, *
    by taking on Christ's self.

5. Love means surrendering our lives to Christ, *
    to take on the richness of his love.

6. Love alone can make the wolf and lamb dwell together; *
    Love alone can so fill the earth
    that death and destruction come to an end.

7. Come to us now, Lord of love; *
    Come and deliver us.

Psalm 55:
What Is It That We Seek

Dorothy Day (1897–1980)

1. What is it that we seek for, every one of us, *
     except to love and be loved?

2. In times of tension and terror, *
     how can we continue to think of love?

3. Yet even the revolutionary seeking to overturn
   the established order, *
     is seeking a world in which love is possible.

4. We want with all our hearts to love and be loved, *
     we long to look on all people as our family.

5. To be in love, so that every thought, word,
   and deed is bathed in love, *
     gives us a taste of the love of God for us
     and the love we should have for all.

6. To love another is to see the good in them, the Christ in them, *
     as God sees Christ in us and loves us.

7. It is easy to talk about love, *
     but love must be tested and proven and learned.

8. It is a terrible thing to see the ugliness of decaying neighborhoods, *
     to see what human beings have made of human life.

9. All things must be restored in Christ: *
    individual bodies and the societies in which we live.

10. We must die to the natural and live in the supernatural; *
    we must do all for the love of God.

Psalm 56:
Paul May Plant

Maria W. Stewart (1803–1880)

1. Paul may plant and Apollos may water, *
    but God alone gives the increase.

2. Without God's help we are nothing; *
    without God's blessing our work is in vain.

3. O Lord our God, you have our hearts in your hand, *
    and you can turn our hearts wherever you will.

4. Strip our hearts from the worship of idols; *
    turn our eyes away from all that is vain.

5. You are able to glorify yourself by making us monuments of your mercy, *
    and you can glorify yourself by making us monuments
    of your wrath; make us monuments of your victorious grace.

6. Open our eyes to see how our feet are set in slippery places, *
    let us see the billows that roll beneath our feet.

7. Have mercy, Lord God, on those who have not known your grace, *
    soften the proud and rebellious hearts.

8. Did you not die, Lord Jesus so that these also might live? *
    Did you not become poor so that they might be rich?
    Is not your blood sufficient to redeem us all?

9. Not alone for ourselves do we pray, gracious God; *
    but for all nations, kindreds, and tongues do we pray.

10. Grant that a host beyond numbering may be gathered in, *
    bring them back from the four winds and the seven seas.

11. Let us hear your voice when the last day comes, *
    saying, "Well done, good and faithful servant;

12. "You have been faithful in a few things, *
    you will be set over many things;
    enter into the joy of your Lord."

Psalm 57:
Permit Me, O Lord

Elizabeth Rowe (1674–1737)

1. Permit me, O Lord God, to plead with you a little; *
    what profit would you have from loss of me?

2. Mercy is your brightest quality; *
    mercy completes your beauty.

3. By kindness and forgiveness you are known; *
    in compassion you reveal yourself to me.

4. But will you indeed forgive me, O my God? *
    Will you restore the standing I have lost?

5. What wondrous love is found in your forgiveness; *
    what astonishing compassion!

6. Almighty love, the theme of heavenly song! *
    Infinite grace, the wonder of the angels!

7. Forgive the mortal tongue that seeks to praise you; *
    if we were silent, the stones would sing instead.

8. O narrow thoughts and yet more narrow words; *
    what language can I find to tell your praise?

9. Infinitely worthy are you, our Lord and God; *
    who shall not praise you and magnify your Name? *

10. We murmur from the dust, yet you listen to our voice; *
    though angels sing your praises, you listen to our complaints.

11. When you are present, hope and heaven follow; *
    in your absence, darkness and despair surround my life.

12. When you are absent, darkness and despair attack me; *
    peace and joy are empty sounds, words lose their meaning.

13. When you are absent, nature cannot repair my loss; *
    heaven and earth offer their treasures in vain.

14. What are disgrace and poverty and pain,
    what are all the fear that mortals experience? *
    All these are nothing compared to the loss of my God.

15. I wait for your return as one watching for the day to dawn; *
    life is meaningless if your glory will not come again!

16. When will you scatter the darkness that conceals you from me? *
    When will the glory of your grace dawn on my mind?

17. When will grief and anxiety vanish before you? *
    When will immortal joy surround my soul?

18. You are a flame which the most glorious part
    of creation cannot equal; *
    without you there is an emptiness only infinite love can fill.

19. You, Lord, are my boundless treasure; *
    you are my infinite delight, my joy beyond words.

20. Show me, O Lord, where you are and lead me into your presence; *
    let your love for me hold me there forever.

Psalm 58:
Lord, What Are We

Richard Crashaw (1613–1649)

1. Lord, what are we that you should pay so high a price? *
    Why should you pay so much for a thing of no value?

2. What difference would it make to you if we did not exist? *
    Heaven would still be heaven
    whether we strode the earth or not.

3. Let us go weep for all our sins; *
    the seraphim will still surround your throne
    and the planets run their courses.

4. Still will the heavens ring with your praise, *
    and the angels burn as brightly as before.

5. Still will thrones and dominions worship you, *
    and archangels sing your praises night and day.

6. Let mortal dust do as it will *
    and let the winds carry that dust where they will.

7. Why should you bow your head to see *
    what my own foolishness has done to me?

8. Why should the king leave the royal throne *
    because some wandering fool has been undone?

9. Will the sun change its course or shine less brightly *
    because some foolish fly has fallen to the ground?

10. What has the Lamb done that deserves death? *
    If the wolf has sinned, why should the Lamb bleed?

11. O dearest Savior, make me see *
    how dearly you have paid for me.

12. As my life has been lost in death, *
    grant that it may be lost in love.

Psalm 59:
Lead Me, Light of God

John Henry Newman (1801–1890)

1. Lead me, Light of God, though darkness surrounds me, *
    though I am far from home, lead me onward.

2. Guide me step by step, one step at a time, *
    I do not need to see the distant goal.

3. I have not always asked your guidance, Lord of light, *
    I have preferred to choose my own path;
    I have looked for other light.

4. Do not remember my former behavior; *
    forgive me my past blindness.

5. You have guided me in my blindness; *
    provided a pathway in the wilderness.

6. Guide me still in the darkness; *
    bring me at last to the true light of everlasting day.

7. In this world of mystery, there is one true Light that guides us; *
    it is light enough for our present needs.

8. Take away this light and we are lost; *
    we know not where we are or what to believe,
    why we exist, or where we are going.

9. With the Light of God we have all we need in abundance; *
    we do not ask for clearer sight or greater wisdom.

10. Let us instead give thanks for God's goodness in time past, *
    for sins forgiven, dangers avoided, prayers answered,
    errors corrected.

11. Let us give thanks for lessons learned and strength provided, *
    for times of trial and times of renewal.

12. Let us give thanks that we have had light enough for our needs, *
    strength enough for the journey.

Psalm 60:
Where Is the Secret Treasure

Jean Pierre de Caussade (1675–1751)

1. Where is the secret treasure to be found? *
    The treasure is everywhere.

2. The treasure is offered to us at every moment; *
    it is to be found wherever we find ourselves.

3. Friends and enemies alike pour out the treasure freely; *
    it courses through every fiber of our being.

4. God's activity runs throughout the universe; *
    if we open our mouth, it will be filled.

5. The treasure penetrates every created being; *
    wherever we are, it is there also.

6. The treasure runs always ahead of us; *
    it stays with us and follows after us.

7. All we need do is let the waves of life sweep us forward *
    and surrender to the will of God in all things.

8. Like a clean canvass, we must offer ourselves to God *
    and let God paint on it whatever it is God wills.

Psalm 61:
The Holy Spirit Leads Me Gently

Mechthild of Magdeburg (1207–c. 1290)

1. The Holy Spirit leads me gently *
    and teaches me all that I need.

2. When wisdom is not grounded in the Spirit, *
    it becomes a mountain of arrogance.

3. When peace is not restrained by the Spirit, *
    it quickly turns to rage.

4. Humility without the fire of love *
    becomes open hypocrisy in the end.

5. Justice that lacks the depth of God's humility *
    quickly turns into dreadful hatred.

6. Poverty, freely chosen, is beautiful, *
    but poverty can be as greedy as wealth.

7. Fine behavior that is a cloak for greed *
    will be obvious to the wise.

8. A true longing for holiness *
    comes to no one without effort.

9. A comfortable life without testing *
    produces little of value.

10. A virtuous life not grounded in God *
    will be brought low by pride.

11. Fine promises without the deeds *
    are falsehoods that come from the devil.

12. Love needs humility for its mother and holy fear for its father *
    or else it is an orphan without any virtue.

Psalm 62:
Deep Within Us

Thomas R. Kelly (1893–1941)

1. Deep within us is a holy place, a divine center *
    to which we may always return.

2. Eternity is in our hearts, *
    it presses against our time-worn lives.

3. Eternity warms us with its echoes of a destiny beyond time, *
    it calls us home to ourselves.

4. We are called to self-surrender and listening, *
    to adoration and joy and thankfulness.

5. In this center of creation, all things are ours, *
    and we are Christ's and Christ is God's.

6. We come to the Light and bring the world with us, *
    we return and bring the Light to the world.

7. In faith we bring all things to the light *
    to see them in a new way
    and respond to them in love and faith.

8. We respond with faith and hope and love, *
    as we learn to see all things as God sees them.

9. Persistence in prayer and inward submission,
    waiting quietly and constantly returning: *
    these are the requirements of growth in the Spirit.

10. The One who begins this work within us *
    can establish it also until we are grounded in love.

Psalm 63:
Let Us With Pure Hearts

Clement of Alexandria (150–215)

1. Let us with pure hearts *
    give praise to the Word who rules us.

2. We who are born of Christ, joined in a choir of peace, *
    let us sing God's praise with untiring voices.

3. We who are nourished by the milk of heaven, *
    with milk distilled from the breast of Reason,

4. Let us join to sing hymns of praise, *
    clear and pure hymns to Christ our Ruler.

5. Bridle of untamed colts, *
    compass of wandering birds,

6. Rudder of great ships, *
    shepherd of straying lambs:

7. Guide of our children, Ruler of the saints, *
    draw your children together.

8. Word of the most high God, *
    ruler of wisdom,

9. Strength of the sorrowful, joy of the ages, *
    Savior of human life,

10. Creator of unending galaxies, *
    who set the stars in their courses,

11. Who set the sea in its place *
    and raised high the mountain peaks,

12. Who sends us the seasons in their turn: *
    the snows of winter and green trees of summer,

13. The fresh flowers of spring-time, *
    and the abundant harvests of autumn,

14. You who brought order out of chaos *
    and set us on earth to seek justice and peace:

15. Grant us the gift of lives spent in your praise; *
    let us be guided in all things by your Word made flesh
    and by the Holy Spirit.

Psalm 64:
Beyond All Else

Alfred Noyes (1880–1958)

1. Beyond all else that is created and further still, *
    what do we go to seek?

2. Is not the heart of all things here and now? *
    Is not the circle infinite but the center everywhere?

3. Come, then, and see the secret of the sun, *
    and the sorrow that holds all things together,
    the pain that holds eternity in an hour.

4. There is one God in every bursting seed, *
    one Christ present in every flower.

5. I will bind up every wound, *
    when all things are restored and renewed.

6. One thing is needed: be true to yourself *
    and the one God who formed you.

7. The day and the night require this one thing only: *
    that you love one another and let your love be strong.

8. And all that is broken shall be mended, *
    and all that is lost shall be found.

Psalm 65:
Strangely You Come

Anna Bunston (1869–1954)

1. Strangely you come, O Lord, beneath my roof, *
    lacking all royal adornment and authority, you come.

2. "Can this be God," I ask myself; *
    the Ruler of the universe, coming to me?

3. God is the Creator of infinite space and beyond all knowing; *
    we are nothing but adopted children,
    slaves redeemed from Satan's power.

4. God is mightier than the mountains, *
    yet comes with no show of power.

5. Yet invisible voices summon me and say, *
    your Savior seeks your poverty.

6. I, the humblest of human beings, *
    am embraced by Love, made partaker of heavenly grace.

7. No invented excuses make me less unworthy; *
    no pretense of humility can earn your attention.

8. Your glorious condescension blazes through my misery; *
    your love finds room enough in my nothingness.

9. My soul is dark, yet you seek me; *
    my night allows your daylight to shine.

10. I am the clay and you are the potter; *
    I am the harp and you are the musician's hand.

11. All the world seeks to draw me away from you, *
    therefore stay with me in my need.

12. Leave me not lest my faith should falter; *
    let me be an acceptable offering to you;
    be to me the consuming fire.

Psalm 66:
Pure Prayer Occurs

Wycliffite Spirituality (14th Century)

1. Pure prayer occurs when the mind ascends to God; *
    when we turn away from self to love of God alone.

2. Pure prayer occurs when what is sought is forgotten; *
    when we know only the love we enjoy.

3. God pays no attention to flowery words and phrases, *
    for the fervent prayer may be rough and simple.

4. Pure prayer is prayer that resonates in joy; *
    pure prayer moves beyond words and names
    to rejoice in God alone.

5. Every word, every scripture, every work done in grace, *
    all alike are prayers when devoutly offered to God.

6. Vocal prayer has the fire of love within it; *
    it reaches forcefully to God out of our misery.

7. Prayer that lacks love does not rise up; *
    it lacks the holy meditation that brings peace.

8. Prayer that lacks the devotion that enkindles fire, *
    is only a stinking smoke.

9. The smoke of burning prayer does not drift upward, *
    but it blinds the eyes of the speaker,
    and leaves us walking in darkness.

10. The fervor of love is a subtle fire; *
    the rarified air is the meditation of heaven.

11. The high and holy One directs us to think on our suffering with sorrow, *
    so we may demand the assistance of God's mercy.

12. To pray without ceasing is to offer the prayer of mercy, *
    and not the prayer of the voice.

13. Those who live in love and do all things with mercy, *
    those are the ones who pray well,
    and those who live best, pray best.

14. Every psalm, every scripture, every work done in grace, *
    all these are prayers devoutly offered to God.

15. Those who pray with a burning desire to serve God
    will have victory over evil; *
    calm, peace, and charity will dwell among them.

16. Let us consider what true purity is, *
    the better to expose our weakness.

17. The blindness caused by our sins, *
    is the greatest reason we neglect our prayers.

18. Those who come before God with a mind on the marketplace and a body in the pew,
    with the hymn on our tongue and our interest in the dance, *
    these are very poorly disposed to move toward God.

19. Let us pray at all times; *
    there is never emptiness in good work.

20. God is the medium that inspires,
    and the fulfillment of the end, *
    God is the fruit that gives rest to the soul.

Psalm 67:
What I Ask For

Dag Hammarskjöld (1905–1961)

1. What I ask for is absurd: *
   that life shall have a meaning.

2. What I strive for is impossible: *
   that my life shall acquire a meaning.

3. I am being driven forward into an unknown land; *
   the air as I climb becomes colder and sharper.

4. A wind from the heights ahead of me, *
   stirs an expectation of the mystery that lies beyond.

5. The question always remains to be answered: *
   will I attain the goal?

6. Will I arrive at the place where life resounds: *
   a pure, clear note in the silence.

7. Day after day, I cannot forget, *
   the days I have lost from my journey.

8. The more faithfully you listen to the voice within, *
   the better you will hear the voice outside.

9. To reach perfection, we must turn away from self; *
   one by one, we must pass through the death to self.

10. Life in God does not set us free from sin, *
    but it opens our eyes to see it.

11. When we can stand in the all-seeing light of love *
    we can look at the evil within us.

12. A living relationship with God is the first necessity; *
    with that we can know ourselves
    and be victorious and forgiven.

13. Do you seek God's glory or your own? *
    The answer determines the outcome of our actions.

14. We must find the peace and balance of mind *
    to give every word of criticism its proper weight
    and humble ourselves before every word of praise.

15. The best and most wonderful gift we are given *
    is the silence in which God speaks.

16. Do not look back and do not fear the future; *
    our reward and our destiny is here and now.

17. It is not for us to ask why it happens or where it may lead; *
    our task is to make use of the moment,
    and there is One who will judge.

18. In your word, in your light, what else is significant? *
    Our happiness is found in that which alone is great.

19. In the faith which is God's marriage to the soul *
    everything has a meaning and purpose.

20. In the faith which is God's marriage to the soul, *
    we are one in God and God is wholly in us
    and wholly in all we meet.

21. How great is all that we are given, *
    and how meaningless all that we must sacrifice.

22. Give us a pure heart to see you, *
    give us a humble heart to hear you;

24. Give us a heart of love to serve you, *
    give us a heart of faith to love you.

Psalm 68:
Like the Sun at Noonday

Dante Alighieri (1265–1321)

1. Like the sun at noonday is your love to us, Lord God, *
    and like a flowing spring from which comes life.

2. Those who seek grace and do not come to you, *
    are like those who hope to fly but have no wings.

3. All goodness that we know, all that is excellent and true, *
    all pity, mercy, and charity find their unity in you.

4. I look to you and have no words to speak, *
    nor can human memory contain the vision we are given.

5. Yet grant my tongue ability to speak and to express *
    some shadow of the glory that blinds our human eyes.

6. Let future generations also know your splendor *
    undimmed by passing time and feeble memory.

7. By grace alone can human vision see, *
    the final glory with unblinded eyes.

8. No human language can express that glory, *
    logic and reason are helpless to understand.

9. No one who sees that radiance can freely turn away, *
    there is no other light that can compare.

10. All truth and goodness are contained within that light, *
    all that is elsewhere incomplete is perfected in its beam.

11. My tongue can no more find the words to use *
    than could an infant at its mother's breast.

12. So in the darkness of that dazzling light, *
    my blinded eye imagines rainbows infinite.

13. O Light eternal, how feeble is human speech, *
    to speak of that which words cannot contain.

14. Yet heart and mind are drawn by love alone, *
    that love that moves the sun and all the stars.

Psalm 69:
How Sweet a Thought

Richard Baxter (1615–1691)

1. How sweet a thought is everlasting rest, *
   the promise of eternal peace.

2. Not as the stone rests on the earth or the flesh in the grave, *
   but a rest from conflict and not from joy.

3. What joy there will be in the presence of God, *
   where love is perfect and joy is complete.

4. Now, blessed saints, who believe and obey, *
   this is the end of your patience and faith.

5. This is the reward of your waiting and prayer, *
   will you regret then the time spent in serving?

6. Look, and see the Judge who looks at you in love, *
   listen, and you will hear your name being called.

7. Hear the invitation to stand at God's right hand, *
   have no fear but go forward and stand by the throne.

8. Unworthy though we are, the crown is held out; *
   this is the wonder of grace freely given,
   this is the climax of eternal love.

9. This is that joy that was purchased by sorrow, *
   this is the crown that was bought by the cross.

10. Where now are the old divisions and conflicts? *
    Where now is the anger that kept us apart?

11. Here we are all of one heart in one everlasting home; *
    here we find unity un-glimpsed before.

12. This new home is not like the houses of clay, *
    which were our earthly habitations.

13. Here the voice that is heard is a song of joy, *
    no longer impatient complaints and groans.

14. This risen body is not like the body we had before, *
    nor is this life like the life we once knew.

15. Where now are our former divisions and conflicts? *
    What condemnations do we hear now?

16. No more, my friend, will you mourn the loss of companions; *
    no longer will you stand in silent mourning at their graves.

17. Here there is no further conflict with Satan; *
    no more will you battle against temptations on every side.

18. Headaches and hunger, fevers and sleeplessness, *
    weakness and exhaustion are banished forever.

19. Farewell now to sin and to sorrows and unbelief; *
    welcome the joy of new life eternal.

20. This is the New Jerusalem, the city of golden light; *
    this is the city of unity and praise.

21. Hasten, O Lord, the coming of that day, *
    let our prayers be answered and the new life begin.

22. Let the vision of that city sustain us day by day, *
    and let our present life be renewed
    and restored by forgiveness and grace.

Psalm 70:
Sun, Moon, and Stars

Alfred, Lord Tennyson (1809–1892)

1. Sun, moon, and stars, the mountains, oceans, and plains, *
    do not these exist because God called them into being?

2. And are not the earth and solid stars and the weight of human life, *
    the Vision of their Creator?

3. Is the world dark to us and God's purpose a mystery? *
    Is it self-knowledge we seek, or the light of God?

4. Glory surrounds us and we seek for the light, *
    stifling the splendor, searching for broken gleams.

5. But if we speak, the Almighty will hear, *
    the Ultimate is closer than breathing,
    and nearer than hands and feet.

6. God is law, says the wise one; let us give thanks: *
    if the law thunders, let us learn to listen.

7. "The law is no God at all," says the fool;
    "all we can see is a dim and broken reflection,

8. And the human ear cannot hear, and the human eye is blind." *
    but the Vision remains and requires a response.

9. You, Almighty God, live in the vast universe you have created *
    and exist beyond space and time.

10. You are able to watch the years pass like moments *
    and see the things that lie beyond the boundaries of our sight.

11. You are able to number the stars in the galaxies; *
    you hold the swirling nebulae in the hollow of your hand.

12. Are You then simply a staring splendor like the sun? *
    Do you not heed the helpless sparrow's fall?

13. Do you not mourn the lost and wandering sheep? *
    Can you not hear the cry of the smallest child
    and watch above them as they sleep?

14. Only in that Ultimate Being can I at last find a home; *
    only with the risen One beside me
    can I face the new day.

Psalm 71:
Eternal Lord and Creator

Sophronius of Jerusalem (560–638)

1. Eternal Lord and Creator of all that is, *
    you have called me into life and sustained me to this day.

2. You have given me the gift of baptism, *
    and strengthened me with the gift of the Spirit.

3. You have placed within me a desire to seek you; *
    therefore listen to my prayer.

4. Apart from you I have no life, no light, no joy, or wisdom; *
    apart from you I have no strength.

5. I have no right to lift my eyes to you, *
    but you have promised to hear my prayer.

6. Purify my mind and my heart, O Lord, *
    and teach me how to pray.

7. By the strength that you alone can give, *
    enable me to speak and act to your glory.

8. Give me the gifts of humility and patience, *
    grant me gentleness, courage, wisdom, and peace.

9. Show me, O Lord, the path of your will, *
    and help me to walk in your sight without sin.

10. All hearts are open to you, Lord God, *
    you know my need before I ask.

11. You know my blindness and ignorance, *
    you know my weakness and my failures.

12. When my self-will leads me down false paths, *
    draw me back, O Lord; compel my obedience.

13. If it is your will that I keep silence, *
    grant me the gift of a peaceful spirit
    to cause no sorrow or hurt to others.

14. Set me on the way of your commandments, *
    and let me not stray before my final breath.

15. Let your will be my only law, *
    both now and to all eternity.

16. In my weakness and foolishness, O God, *
    I ask you for many and great gifts,

17. Yet I am always aware of my weaknesses and sins, *
    cast me not away from your presence.

18. Grant me such grace, O Lord, that I may love you as you command: *
    with all my heart and mind and soul and strength.

19. Do not take me away in the midst of my days, *
    nor while my mind is still blind.

20. Give me an answer, Lord, before your judgment seat *
    and grant me the joy of your salvation.

Psalm 72:
You the Creator

William Barclay (1907–1978)

1. You, the Creator, have made all things and made them well; *
    we praise you for the world in which we live;

2. We thank you for the light of the day *
    and the dark times of rest,

3. For the glory of the sunlight, *
    and the silvery splendor of the moon
    and for the star-scattered sky,

4. For the gentle hills and the soaring mountains, *
    and the rolling waves of the sea,

5. For the city streets and the country roads, *
    for the deep forests and open plains.

6. We thank you, Lord God, for the life you have given us, *
    and the work you have given us to do.

7. We thank you for eyes to see and ears to hear, *
    for minds to think and hearts to love.

8. We thank you for families and friends, *
    and the colleagues with whom we work.

9. We thank you for memories of the years that are past, *
    and for minds to envision the gift of years to come.

10. Praise and glory and worship we offer you, our Lord, *
    in whom we live and who has offered us life forever.

Psalm 73: You Are Risen

Eric Milner-White (1884–1963)

1. You are risen, O Lord; let the trumpets shout salvation; *
   let the news run like holy fire to the ends of the earth.

2. You are risen, O Lord; let all creation shout the tidings; *
   the long night is past and the Savior is alive!

3. You are risen, O Lord; let us come to rise with you; *
   let us come to receive you with wonder and joy.

4. You are risen, O Lord; let my heart rise up with you; *
   come to me also in spite of closed doors.

5. Show me your hands and side so I may truly see you; *
   send me to serve you here and forever.

6. Bring us to the dawning of that day, *
   when we will live with you in the resurrection life.

7. Show me, O God most holy, in the measure of mortal sight, *
   the splendor of your power, wisdom, and love;

8. As the sun breaks upon the night shadows, and day leaps into joy, *
   let us see your glory, the glory by which we live.

9. You have revealed your glory in the face of a little child; *
   you have made known your glory in one dying alone; *

10. Bring me to the everlasting goal: *
    the sight of your glory in the light of your face.

Psalm 74:
Enter My Heart

Eric Milner-White (1884–1963)

1. Enter my heart, Holy Spirit, *
   to break the bonds of sin.

2. Bring me out of the prison of old habits and false desires, *
   free me from the pattern of indolence and self-will.

3. Come, Holy Spirit, in your mercy, *
   empower me and set me free.

4. Throw open the locked gates of my mind, *
   cleanse the chambers of my thoughts
   and make your home within.

5. Plant the seed of new understanding, *
   and nourish new growth in wisdom.

6. Light within me the fire of your own holy brightness, *
   and give me a vision of your purpose for human society.

7. Come, Holy Spirit, and unshackle my inner life; *
   free me from the dungeon of inertia and despair.

8. O Holy Spirit, whose presence is liberty, *
   grant me the perfect freedom of perfect obedience.

9. Come, most Holy Spirit, possess me with your peace; *
   illuminate me with your truth and fire me with your flame.

10. Enable me by your power, *
    make visible the fruit of your presence within.

11. Lift me by grace upon grace, *
    raise me from glory to glory.

12. Come, Holy Spirit, in your mercy, *
    empower me and set me free.

Psalm 75:
I Do Not Need Any Hope

Simone Weil (1909–1943)

1. I do not need any hope or promise *
    to believe that God is rich in mercy.

2. I know the wealth of God's mercy with the certainty of experience; *
    I have touched it.

3. What I know of God's mercy through actual contact
   is so far beyond my understanding and gratitude *
    that not even the promise of future bliss can add to it.

4. Human mercy is shown only in giving joy; *
    God's mercy is manifest in affliction as well as joy.

5. If we persevere in love in the depths of affliction, *
    we touch something that is neither affliction or joy,
    but the love of God itself.

6. We know that joy is the sweetness of contact with God's love, *
    and affliction is the pain of that contact;

7. But only the contact with God's love matters; *
    and not the manner of it.

8. The knowledge of the presence of God affords no consolation,
   nor does it remove the bitterness of affliction, *
    but God's love for us is the substance of the bitterness.

9. Even if there were nothing more for us than earthly life,
even if death brings us nothing new, *
   the superabundance of divine mercy is already secretly present here below in its entirety.

10. If I were to fall to the bottom of hell,
I should already owe God an infinite debt of gratitude, *
   for God's infinite mercy in my earthly life.

11. Already here below we are given the capacity to love God *
   and know that in God are found eternal and infinite joy.

12. Through the veil of the flesh we receive from above, *
   evidence enough of eternity to silence any doubt.

13. What more can we ask or desire? *
   What we have is perfect joy.

14. All that is left to hope for *
   is grace to be obedient.

Psalm 76:
Thousands and Thousands of Years

Christopher Fry (1907–2005)

1. Thousands and thousands of years lie behind us, vexed and terrible, *
    and still we turn for healing to the cures that have never healed.

2. Think of the wisdom, admired but not followed; *
    think of the wings that have never been used,
    still folded in the heart.

3. Good has no fear; it faces whatever comes, *
    it grows and persuades.

4. Why do we trust the powers that destroy us, *
    and not the power that renews us and recreates?

5. Good is stronger than anger and wiser than strategy, *
    good can subdue armies if we believe it with courage.

6. The old measures will never bring us to the morning, *
    expedience and self-preservation will rot and decay.

7. The human heart can go the lengths of God, *
    dark and cold we may be, but winter comes to an end.

8. The frozen misery of centuries breaks, cracks, and begins to move, *
    the thunder we hear is the upstart Spring.

9. Thank God our time is now, *
    when evil comes up to face us everywhere;

PSALM 76: THOUSANDS AND THOUSANDS OF YEARS 137

10. Never to leave us until we take the longest stride of soul *
    that human beings ever took.

11. The enterprise to which we are called *
    is exploration into God.

Psalm 77:
Truth Beyond All Truth

Lancelot Andrewes (1555–1626)

1. Truth beyond all truth, reality beyond all reality, *
    Maker of all worlds that exist,

2. I set you before my face *
    and lift my heart to you.

3. I worship you on my knees *
    and humble myself beneath your strong hand.

4. Source of all mercy, I beseech your affection; *
    do not despise the work of your own hands.

5. Lord, if you will, you can make me clean; *
    say only the word and I shall be cleansed.

6. Savior of sinners, of whom I am the chief, *
    do not despise the cost of your blood,
    I who am called by your Name.

7. Look at me with those same eyes, *
    that looked at Peter in the judgment hall
    and the thief on the cross.

8. Remember me, Lord, in your kingdom, *
    and let me hear you say, "Your sins are forgiven."

9. All-holy, good, and Life-giving Spirit, *
    breathe in me the breath of life,

10. Turn again, my Savior, at the last, *
    and be gracious to your servant.

Psalm 78:
Consider the Treasure Within

William Law (1686–1761)

1. Consider, poor sinner, the treasure you have within, *
    the eternal Word of God lies hidden within you.

2. A spark of the Divine Nature which is to overcome sin and death *
    is able to generate the life of Heaven in your soul.

3. Turn to your heart and your heart will find *
    its Savior within itself.

4. You see and hear and feel nothing of God *
    because you seek for God with your outward eyes.

5. You seek God in books and controversy, *
    in the church and outward exercises,

6. But you will not find God in the outward world *
    for God must be found first in the heart.

7. Seek for God in the heart *
    and you will never seek in vain,

8. For God dwells in the heart; *
    that is the seat of God's light and the Holy Spirit.

9. This turning to the light and the Spirit of God within *
    is the only true turning to God.

10. There is no other way of finding God *
    than to go to that place within where God dwells.

11. God is, of course, present everywhere *
    but God is present to you
    only in the deepest, most central part of your soul.

12. The natural senses cannot possess God *
    nor can they unite you to God.

13. Even the inward faculties of understanding and will and memory *
    can only reach after God,
    but cannot be the place of God's dwelling within.

14. There is a root or depth from which these faculties come forth *
    as branches come from the trunk of the tree.

15. This depth is called the center of the soul *
    and nothing can satisfy it except the infinity of God.

16. Awake then from your sleep *
    and Christ will give you light.

17. Search and dig in the field of your soul *
    for the pearl of eternity lying within.

18. When the first spark of desire for God rises in your soul *
    cherish it with all care and give your whole heart to it.

19. Get up and follow gladly *
    as the Wise Men followed the star.

20. It will lead you to the birth of Jesus,
    not in a stable at Bethlehem *
    but in the dark center of your fallen soul.

Psalm 79:
I Would Like to Be Free

Karl Rahner (1904–1984)

1. I would like to be a person who is free and able to hope *
   who exists at the mercy of freedom.

2. I am convinced that a human being's life moves in freedom toward a decision; *
   I believe that life as a whole must be answered for.

3. I do not try to escape from myself *
   or to flee from the responsibility of freedom.

4. I accept my existence in hope; *
   I believe that the ultimate meaning of life will be revealed
   at last in joy.

5. I commit myself to an unconditional hope, *
   a hope that supports everything else that I do.

6. I do not commit myself to a faith that provides final answers, *
   but I acknowledge a mystery beyond my understanding.

7. God is the beginning and end of my hope,
   the mystery to whom we respond in worship.

8. God is the beginning and end of my hope, *
   God alone is my salvation.

9. Even in the darkness and disappointment of life, *
    life begins to emerge in beauty
    and everything becomes promise.

10. Time goes by and the mystery does not yet dawn as happiness, *
    but it is better to wait in patience for the day
    that will never end.

Psalm 80:
God Is Not Loved Without Reward

Bernard of Clairvaux (1090–1153)

1. God is not loved without reward, *
    though reward should not be our motive.

2. Love is an affection, but not a contract;
    it is not given or received by agreement.

3. Love must be freely given; *
    it finds its reward in giving, not receiving.

4. A reward is offered to the one who does not yet love, *
    and given to the one who perseveres.

5. The one who truly loves God asks no reward except God; *
    the one who asks for more does not love God.

6. Earthly ambition is never satisfied; *
    we seek always the highest and best and are never satisfied.

7. We build houses worthy of a king and add house to house, *
    we knock down and build again,
    restlessly seeking something better.

8. We seek endlessly for something better, *
    and seldom take time to enjoy what we have.

9. We lust after new experiences and possessions, *
    and seek not the Creator of all.

10. The desire to possess everything is a winding road, *
    it circles endlessly and never arrives at its goal.

11. Yet there are some who have no need to possess whatever they see, *
    but even sell what they have and give it to the poor.

12. God stirs us to goodness; anticipates, sustains, fulfills; *
    it is God who causes us to desire,
    and God alone who satisfies that desire.

Psalm 81:
You Promised, Lord

Bernard of Clairvaux (1090–1153)

1. You promised, Lord, that we will see you soon, *
    but it is too long, O Lord; it seems too long.

2. It may be short in terms of what we deserve, *
    but it is long in terms of our desire.

3. Those who love God are carried away by longing, *
    we are swept away by our desire.

4. Those who love God close their eyes to the glory *
    and trust in God's saving grace.

5. I will tell you my own experience; *
    the Word has come even to me,
    and come to me more than once.

6. I have never been aware of that coming, *
    I have known the presence of the Word
    and remembered that presence afterward.

7. Sometimes I have been aware of the coming of the Word, *
    but I have never felt the coming, nor been aware of the leaving.

8. Where the Word comes from I do not know, *
    nor do I know where the Word goes in leaving.

9. The Word does not enter by the eye, for the Word has no color; *
    nor does the Word enter by the ear, for there is no sound.

10. The Word does not come from within me, *
     for there is no good in me, but the Word is good.

11. I have climbed as high as I can, but the Word is far, far higher; *
     I have plumbed my own depths, but the Word is deeper still.

12. How then do I know the presence *
     of the One whose ways cannot be traced?

13. The Word is life and power, * and stirs my sleeping soul.

14. That Word soothes and pierces my heart *
     which was hard as stone and riddled with disease.

15. The Word begins to root up and destroy, *
     to build again and to plant,

16. To water the dry places and light the dark corners, *
     to open what was closed, and set what was cold on fire,

17, So my soul gives praise to the Lord, *
     and all my heart gives praise.

18. So when the Word came to me, *
     there was no sight or sound of that coming,

19. And none of my senses revealed *
     what flooded the depths of my being.

20. But I knew by the warmth of my heart, *
     that the yearnings of my body were controlled.

21. At the slightest sign of amendment of life, *
     I experience the goodness of God's mercy.

22. When I contemplate all these things *
     I am filled with awe at God's glory.

Psalm 82:
How Can I Serve You

John Baillie (1886–1960)

1. How can I serve you, gracious God, *
    when I am so prone to seek my own will:

2. So much attached to the pleasures of the senses, *
    so negligent of the things of the spirit,

3. So quick to gratify my body, *
    so slow to nourish my soul,

4. So greedy for present delights, *
    so indifferent to everlasting blessedness,

5. So fond of leisure time, *
    so reluctant to do my work,

6. So often found at play, *
    so seldom found at prayer,

7. So ready to serve myself, *
    so slow to seek to serve others,

8. So eager to get more for myself, *
    so reluctant to share it with others,

9. So full of good intentions, *
    so empty of accomplishment,

10. So critical of my neighbors and friends, *
    so ready to excuse myself,

11. So helpless apart from your strengthening hand, *
    yet so reluctant to reach out for the help I need.

12. Forgive me, merciful God, *
    and draw me closer to your heart of love.

Psalm 83:
Let Us Seek to Enlarge Our Souls

Lucretia Mott (1793–1880)

1. Let us seek to enlarge our souls; *
   let us approach the Most High in prayer and praise.

2. The truth of God and the righteousness of God: *
   these alone can set us free.

3. Only those who do justice and love righteousness
   offer true worship, *
   those who despise the gains of oppression
   and do not close their eyes to human need.

4. Mighty powers are at work in the world,
   and who shall prevent them? *
   God's word has gone forth and will not return void.

5. Amid the jarrings and commotions and bloodshed, *
   there is a need for workers to face the evils with knowledge
   and faith.

6. Let us rejoice that so many commit themselves to peace; *
   let us give thanks for those who seek
   to end oppression and violence.

7. The kingdom of God is found not in miracles and mysteries, *
   but in righteousness and peace and joy in the Holy Spirit.

8. The blessing of God rests on those who practice mercy
and love and benevolence, *
   who continually hunger for righteousness.

9. Let us seek for peace and love instead of hatred and sword; *
   let us turn to justice and mercy in place of cruelty and oppression.

10. Those who abide in the spirit of the Lord understand true liberty; *
    those who are faithful in their day
    can rest assured that their prayers will be heard.

Psalm 84:
Now Let Us Sing the Eternal Life

Dionysius the Areopagite (5th to 6th Century)

1. Now let us sing the eternal life, *
    the source from which all life comes.

2. Let us sing of the good and eternal life *
    beyond all wisdom and knowledge.

3. Trinity beyond being, beyond divinity and goodness, *
    show us the way to the knowledge beyond wisdom.

4. Fill sightless minds with a brightness beyond all beauty; *
    let us enter the darkness beyond all brightness.

5. Let us pray to enter the dazzling darkness, *
    and through not seeing and not knowing
    let us come to see and to know
    the invisible one beyond all knowing.

6. For the Cause of all things is above every definition, *
    and is freed from all and beyond the whole.

7. Having neither shape nor form, neither seen nor unseen, *
    beyond all knowing, yet known in all things.

8. The all-perfect Cause of all is beyond all human language, *
    yet speaks to us in the Word made flesh.

Psalm 85:
Love Is More Precious Than Gold

John of Forde (c. 1145–1214)

1. Come, then, and let us be on fire with holy love; *
    let us follow the Spirit along the pathway of faith.

2. Love is as precious as gold; *
    it is solid yet filled with light.

3. When Jesus sat down at the right hand of God *
    he sent down love in the hearts of his elect.

4. Love is the pearl of great price, *
    which is gained by selling all else.

5. Love is full of light *
    and reveals the darkness of sin.

6. Love reveals the way of holiness *
    in the beams of its brightness.

7. Love contains in itself an everlasting source, *
    and a power of shining with a glorious natural splendor.

8. That which we see externally is bright, *
    but brighter still is that which lies within.

9. Love frees itself from the things of earth, *
    and is drawn ever upward to heaven.

10, Love, like gold, spreads when it is hammered *
    and is purified by the fire.

11. When love, like gold, is beaten, *
    its inner brightness bursts into view.

12. Through suffering and endurance love constantly grows brighter; *
    it attains the victory and triumph.

Psalm 86:
Christ Is the King of Glory

Martin Luther (1483–1546)

1. Christ is the King of glory, rising from the dead, *
    here the heart can find its supreme joy
    and everlasting possessions.

2. Here is that furnace of love and the fire of love, *
    for Christ is not only born to us,
    but also given to us.

3. By his resurrection he has destroyed sin and raised
   up righteousness, *
    he has abolished death and restored life,
    he has conquered hell and given us everlasting glory.

4. These blessings are so incalculable *
    that the mind of man hardly dares believe
    they have been given us.

5. So Christians may glory in the merits of Christ and all his blessings, *
    as if they themselves had won them.

6. Such a great thing is faith, such blessings does it bring us, *
    such glorious children of God does it make us!

7. We cannot be children of God *
    without receiving God's blessing.

8. Who has conquered sin and death; *
    was it our life or our righteousness?

9. No, it was Jesus Christ, rising from death, *
 condemning sin and death,

10. Bestowing his merits on us, *
 and holding his hand over us.

11. Now all is well with us; *
 sin and death are vanquished.

12. For all this let there be honor, praise, and thanksgiving, *
 to God for ever and ever. Amen.

13. This then is the image that lifts us up, *
 over our evils and even our blessings.

14. We are set down in the midst of blessings, *
 in the righteousness of Christ,

15. Who intercedes for us as our mediator, *
 and gives himself wholly as our high priest and protector.

16. So a Christian becomes almighty lord of all, *
 having all things and doing all things, yet without sin.

17. So we can even glory in our tribulations, *
 scarcely feeling them for the joy we have in Christ.

18. May Jesus Christ, blessed for evermore, *
 instruct us in such glorying. Amen.

Psalm 87:
When I Searched for the Meaning

Hilary of Poitiers (315–367)

1. When I searched for the meaning of life, *
    I sought first for leisure and wealth.

2. But we soon learn there is little satisfaction in those; *
    and the gratifying of greed is unworthy of our humanity.

3. We are given the gift of life to achieve something worthwhile,
    and to make good use of our talents, *
    for life itself points toward a higher realm.

4. Life is painful and full of anxiety; *
    it begins and ends in weakness.

5. Does not our very nature urge us to raise our sights; *
    do we not instinctively know that a good life
    is only gained by good deeds and good actions?

6. Could the immortal God have given us life with no end but death? *
    could the giver of life expect us to live well
    while we are overshadowed always by the fear of death?

7. So I sought to know the One who has given us the gift of life *
   in whose service is found meaning,
   and in whose promise is my hope.

8. My life became filled with the desire *
   to know this God who gives life and meaning.

9. I found some who teach that there are many gods, *
   and some who say there is no God at all.

10. Then I learned that Moses and the prophets bore witness *
    to One who said, "I AM WHO I AM."

11. So I understood that God is Being without end or beginning, *
    and I learned that there is no space without God.

12. I saw that God embraces all that is *
    and encompasses all that exists.

13. So I enjoyed the contemplation of the mystery of God *
    and the wonder of the majesty of God.

14. I worshiped the eternal greatness of my Creator *
    and I longed to behold God's beauty.

15. Then I learned that the eternal Word became flesh
    and dwelt among us; *
    I learned that those who come to God become God's children.

16. So I discovered a greater hope than I had ever imagined: *
    a gift of God freely offered to all.

17. By means of flesh I drew nearer to God *
    and by my faith I came to new birth.

18. By faith I received the gift of freedom, *
    and was empowered to receive a new birth from on high.

Psalm 88:
Weigh All My Faults

Christina Rossetti (1830–1894)

1. Weigh all my faults, O gracious God, *
    weigh all that I have done and left undone;

2. Fashion a scale to weigh them in *
    and pile them, pile them high on your fair scale.

3. Then set my sharp-eyed accuser there to see *
    all that can be recorded to my charge.

4. Let judgment now begin, here in this life *
    and make it evident how far from you I am.

5. And let the whole world see how hard it is *
    to win one solitary, sinful soul to you.

6. I have no merits that might balance all this weight, *
    no, all my work and busy days are useless here.

7. What answer can I make to the accusing voice *
    that knows me, knows me through and through.

8. Yet, gracious God, one drop of blood on Calvary *
    outweighs my guilt, my foolishness, my heart of stone.

Psalm 89:
Peace Does Not Come from Terror

Oscar Romero (1917–1980)

1. Peace does not come from terror or fear; *
   peace is not the silence of cemeteries.

2. Peace is not the silent result of violent repression; *
   peace is not merely the absence of war.

3. Peace is generous and tranquil; *
   peace is the contribution of all to the good of all.

4. Peace is dynamism; *
   peace is generosity.

5. Peace is human right and duty; *
   in peace each one has a place as part of a family.

6. Human beings long for peace and for justice, *
   we long for the reign of God's law;

7. We long for something holy, *
   a new world which we see at a distance.

8. Let us not tire of proclaiming love; *
   love is the force that will overcome the world.

9. Let us not tire of preaching love, *
   though we are overwhelmed with waves of violence
   that only love can overcome.

10. Without love, justice is only a sword; *
    with love, justice becomes a friend's embrace.

11. Without love, laws are arduous and oppressive; *
    with love, law becomes a guiding light.

12. All pomp, all triumph, all selfishness will pass away; *
    what does not pass away is love.

13. The joy of sharing does not pass away; *
    in the end we are judged on love.

Psalm 90:
I Was Felled to the Ground

Anonymous (c. 7th Century)

1. I was felled to the ground *
    at the forest's edge,

2. Severed from my roots *
    and seized by my enemies.

3. Shoulder-high they carried me *
    and set me on a high hill.

4. They made me a mock of scorn *
    for criminals to be mounted on.

5. Many were the malefactors *
    made to suffer on my wood.

6. Then came the king of all *
    with courage to climb me.

7. How would I dare defy, *
    or fail to obey him?

8. I might have felled his foes *
    yet firmly I stood there.

9. I was seized by horror *
    when the hero clasped me.

10. But I dared not bow down *
    or let my boughs bend.

11. So I was raised on high *
    to bear the royal body.

12. They drove dark nails through me, *
    the dire wounds are still visible.

13. They taunted the two of us; *
    a torrent of blood poured down.

14. High on that dark hill, *
    helplessly I suffered.

15. At last thick clouds covered *
    the corpse of the world's savior.

16. The long day was darkened *
    by deep shadows at mid-day.

17. All the clouds gathered *
    and all creation cried in anguish.

18. All this I witnessed: *
    the world changed forever.

Psalm 91:
Eternal Joy and Blessing

Anonymous (14th Century)

1. Eternal joy and blessing comes not from a wealth of things, *
    but comes from the One in whom is unity.

2. Eternal joy and blessing is rooted in God alone; *
    the one and only God must find a home within each one.

3. God is known in all good things, *
    and God is above all good things.

4. Blessedness does not depend on any created thing
   or any work we have done, *
    but only on God and the work that God has done.

5. Therefore I should wait always for God and God's work, *
    and leave aside all creatures and their works,
    and first of all my own self.

6. No great wonders and works of God, not even the Holy God, *
    bring blessing if they remain outside me.

7. God must find a place within me, *
    as a happening, as an inner knowledge,
    as feeling, as taste, as love.

8. Those who live in the Light perceive that all they desire *
    is nothing compared to what is present already,
    in the depth of their being.

9. We long to find sweetness and pleasure, *
    and having it believe we have found God.

10. Then, when the experience is withdrawn,
    we become greatly distressed, *
       we forget God and imagine that all is lost.

11. The true lover of God loves God equally in having or not having; *
    in wealth or in want, in sweetness or bitterness.

12. Let all those who would come to God, *
    search themselves in truth.

Psalm 92:
You, Lord, Have Loved Me

Marguerite Porete (d. 1310)

1. You, Lord, have loved me as Father, *
    in all your everlasting power.

2. You, Lord, have loved me as Son, *
    in all your goodness as a Friend.

3. You, Lord, have loved me as Spirit, *
    in all your everlasting wisdom.

4. This is why Love looks on me and loves no other more than me: *
    the essence of my heart.

5. This is why Love looks on me and this is all Love wants to be: *
    made one with all I am.

6. This is why Love looks on me and loves no other more than me: *
    Love is all I need.

7. This is why Love looks on me: I want what Love wants for me: *
    Love to win my heart.

8. This is why Love looks on me and loves no other more than me – *
    to see Love is my delight.

9. This is why Love looks on me: Love's will is what my will must be; *
    I have no other need.

10. This is why Love looks on me and loves no other more than me: *
    so be it, Love. Amen.

Psalm 93:
Understand and Consider Aright

Jacob Boehme (1575–1624)

1. Understand and consider aright, O mortal, *
    the Eternal One has neither beginning nor end,
    neither height nor depth.

2. Those who approach the Source of life in humility *
    will find virtue and power and life and strength;

3. For the Word of the Lord is the Heart of God *
    where the fountain of the eternal song of praise is found.

4. Yet none can speak of the infinite Source *
    for in that Source is no beginning or end.

5. Lift up your hearts and minds; ride on the chariot of life; *
    look on yourself and all created things,
    and consider the Source of all.

6. You see and feel and find that there is a higher Root; *
    all things come from that invisible and hidden Root.

7. Open your mind and seek and search further; *
    God alone is the Light, God alone is Life.

8. Consider, O human child, the gifts you have been given; *
    do not put out the Eternal Light that burns within.

9. God is a flaming fire, giving light to the world, *
    and in that light is the image and likeness of God.

10. The burning light is sweetened with the essence of love, *
    and this is the cause of nature and of life.

11. May the open fountain in the heart of Jesus Christ refresh us; *
    may that fountain lead us to him that we may live in his power.

12. Let us rejoice in the power of Christ; *
    so that we may love and understand one another,
    and come to a unified will.

Psalm 94:
The Lord of Hosts Protects Us

Desiderius Erasmus (1466–1536)

1. The Lord of hosts protects us; *
   God raises up a people.

2. No one can say, "My King and My God," *
   except with the voice of faith.

3. No one can say, "Jesus is Lord," *
   except by the Holy Spirit.

4. If we call God our ruler, *
   let us obey God's laws.

5. If we call God our ruler, *
   let us love no one more than God.

6. Blessed are those who entrust their lives to God; *
   they have found the purpose for which they were made.

7. This is the purpose for which we were made: *
   to know, to praise, and to love
   our Maker, Redeemer, Reward.

8. Praise in the mouths of sinners has no beauty, *
   nor is singing beautiful that is out of tune.

9. Let us praise God as the angels do *
   among whom there is no division.

10. Let us unite in praise of God, *
    from whom comes all our life.

Psalm 95:
I Have Seen a Mountain

Mechthild of Magdeburg (1207–1290)

1. I have seen a mountain whose foot was cloudy white, *
    and the peak of the mountain was bright as the fiery sun.

2. I can not see the beginning of the mountain, *
    and I cannot see its end.

3. Within itself the mountain shines like molten gold, *
    it shines like love beyond words.

4. Then I said, "Blessed are the eyes that see this flowing love, *
    and bear witness to this wonder."

5. Then the mountain said,
    "The eyes that would see me need seven things; *
    without them they cannot see.

6. "They must borrow reluctantly and pay back willingly *
    and keep nothing for themselves. *

7. "They must meet anger with goodness and violence with love, *
    they must be free of guilt and ready to receive."

Psalm 96:
You Are the One

Geoffrey Studdert-Kennedy (1883–1929)

1. You are the one who dwells in depths of timeless being; *
    you see the years as passing moments;

2. You see the things that lie beyond our vision, *
    the things that are unchanged and constant
    while ages and aeons pass us by.

3. You are the One who can number the stars in their courses, *
    and hold them in your governing hand.

4. You are the Ruler of the universe with its varied forces; *
    the stars and planets are like grains of sand in your sight.

5. Are you then so great that the cries of human pain *
    cannot reach your ears?

6. Are you too distant to know the aching pain of the hungry
   or the tears of the homeless? *
    Are you, like the rich and powerful,
    unconcerned with the needs of the poor?

7. If a thousand years in your sight
    are like the brief moments of our days, *
        can you watch our struggles without concern,
        can you look down with the cold indifference of the moon?

8. Are not even the wild animals in your sight, *
        and do you not notice even the falling sparrow?

9. How then can you ignore the tears of the refugee, *
        do you not watch over us even as we sleep?

10. Are you then too remote to keep me in your sight? *
        Could I alone be beyond your parental care?

11. Only the One who was born in a manger can know my life; *
        only the One who was crucified can understand my fears.

12. You alone can hear the prayers I offer; *
        you alone will stand beside me day by day.

Psalm 97:
How Well I Know

John of the Cross (1542–1591)

1. How well I know the rushing flow of the fountain, *
    even though its eternal spring is hidden.

2. I am able to guess the fountain's source, *
    I can search for it even by night.

3. No one knows the source, nor does it have one, *
    but all that has being comes from that origin.

4. Although it is night, I know there is nothing else so beautiful, *
    earth and heaven find constant refreshment there.

5. I know it has a depth that can never be plumbed, *
    nor is there any ford where it can be crossed.

6. Although it is night, there are no clouds to conceal its clarity, *
    and from it comes the light by which alone we can see.

7. The stream swells up against the banks that strive to confine it, *
    all nations of the earth drink from that stream.

8. Although it is night, I know the current's force is implacable, *
    new streams flow constantly from the eternal source.

9. The eternal source hides in the living Bread, *
    even in the darkness we are fed and nourished.

10. It cries out to all creatures, even by night, *
    "Come and be fed; be nourished and renewed."

11. It cries out to all creation, even by night, *
    "Come and drink your fill of the water of life."

12. This is the living fountain and the bread of life, *
    I see it clearly, although it is night.

Psalm 98:
Come Now, My Friends

Anselm of Canterbury (1033–1109)

1. Come now, my friends, put aside your affairs, *
    escape for a while the tumult of your thoughts.

2. Put aside weighty concerns, *
    leave wearisome toils for another day.

3. Abandon yourself for a little while to God *
    and find rest in your Creator.

4. Go now into the inner chamber of your soul *
    and shut out all other concerns and cares.

5. Speak now to God with your whole heart; *
    say to God, I seek to see your face.

6. Come then, O Lord, and teach my heart: *
    where shall I seek for you? Where shall I find you?

7. If you are not present here, where shall I look for you? *
    If you are present everywhere, why do I not see you?

8. How sad beyond all description is our human lot: *
    how hard and cruel our fall from grace.

9. We have lost the blessedness for which we were made *
    and we have found the misery for which we were not made.

10. You have given me everything that I possess *
    and yet I do not know you.

11. I was created so that I might see you *
    and I have failed to accomplish the purpose
    for which I was made.

12. I was made for the light of your presence, *
    yet I live in darkness and confusion.

13. We have been driven from our homeland into exile; *
    from the vision of God into our present blindness.

14. I yearned for God, but I was in my own way; *
    I looked for peace within myself, but found sadness in my
    heart.

15. How long, O Lord, will you neglect us? *
    When will you look at us and listen to our prayers?

16. I come to you as one who is famished; *
    do not turn me away without food.

17. I come to you as one who is merciful; *
    do not let me be scorned and return with empty hands.

18. I cannot find you unless you teach me how; *
    I cannot find you unless you reveal yourself to me.

19. I do not seek to understand in order to believe, *
    but I believe so I will be able to understand.

19. Let me find you in loving you; *
    let me love you in finding you.

Psalm 99:
God of Justice and Truth

Anselm of Canterbury (1033–1109)

1. God of justice and truth, *
    how can you spare the wicked?

2. How can the One who is supremely just *
    do something unjust?

3. How can you give everlasting life *
    to those who merit eternal death?

4. Since your goodness is beyond our understanding, *
    is the secret of your justice hidden in light inaccessible?

5. Truly the secret of your goodness is hidden *
    in the source from which your mercy flows.

6. We are left to wonder at the mercy *
    that bestows good things on those who are mired in sin.

7. Surely the One who is merciful to the good and the wicked alike *
    is better than one who is merciful only to the good.

8. O fountain of mercy, flowing out in abundance, *
    how boundless is your goodness to us,
    how great should be our love for you!

9. You save the just whom justice commends, *
    and set free the sinful whom justice condemns.

10. O boundless goodness, surpassing all understanding, *
    let your mercy come to me from your great abundance.

11. Truly, if you are merciful because you are supremely good,
    and if you are good only because you are supremely just, *
    then you are merciful because you are supremely just.

12. Help me, just and merciful God, whose light I seek, *
    help me to understand something beyond my understanding.

13. Have you found, O my soul, what you were seeking? *
    But if you have found that light and wisdom and eternal blessedness,
    why do you not experience what you have found?

14. Lord my God, You who have formed and reformed me, *
    tell my soul what you are so I may see what I desire.

15. Truly, Lord you dwell in inaccessible light *
    and nothing can penetrate that light to find you.

16. I am dazzled by your splendor, overcome by your fulness, *
    I am overwhelmed by your immensity.

17. O supreme and inaccessible light, *
    how distant you are from my sight,
    though you see me as I am.

18. You are wholly present everywhere yet I do not see you, *
    in you I live and move, yet I cannot come near you.

19. My God and my Lord, my hope and the joy of my heart, *
    I find in you a joy that is complete and more than complete.

20. I pray, O God, that I may know you and love you and rejoice in you, *
    and if I cannot do so fully in this life,
    let your love grow in me here and be made complete
    in the life to come.

21. Let my mind meditate on that joy, let my tongue speak of it; *
    let my heart love that joy and let my mouth proclaim it;

22. Let my soul hunger for the joy of your presence, *
    and let me enter at last into the joy of the Lord.

Psalm 100:
I Saw a Tree in the Winter

Brother Lawrence of the Resurrection (1614–1691)

1. I saw a tree in the winter stripped of its leaves *
    and I thought that in a little time the leaves would be renewed
    and flowers and fruit would appear.

2. Then I thought so highly of the power and presence of God *
    that it always remains with my soul.

3. Let us establish ourselves in a sense of God's presence *
    and hold conversation constantly with our Creator.

4. Let us feed and nourish our souls
    with the thought of God's presence, *
    and that will yield us great joy.

5. Let us give ourselves up entirely to God *
    and seek satisfaction in the doing of God's will.

6. Let us be governed always by love, *
    and make the love of God the purpose of all that we do.

7. I cannot serve you, Lord, unless you enable me, *
    but your strength is always enough.

8. When I fail, I acknowledge my faults; *
    without God, I will always fall short.

9. When I do not fail, I must give God thanks, *
    for that is always God's doing.

10. Give me a heart that seeks only to serve God, *
    to love nothing but God, and to love God only.

Psalm 101:
Where, Then, Am I Called to Go

John Bunyan (1628–1688)

1. Where, then, am I called to go, I asked, *
    and how shall I find the way?

2. Look for the light, said the man, *
    and enter in at the gate,

3. For there is an endless kingdom to be found, *
    and everlasting life within it.

4. There are crowns of glory to be given us, *
    and garments that shine like the sun.

5. There will be no crying or sorrow there, *
    and every tear shall be wiped away.

6. Yes, said the worldly wise, but in the way there is danger, *
    painfulness, weariness, darkness, and death.

7. Seek then for safety, friendship, and contentment, *
    and make your home with honest neighbors.

8. Some seek to find the way by human wisdom, *
    and some seek their own convenience.

9. But the way of the gospel is narrow and straight, *
    and its walls are called salvation.

10. And though the way is sometimes dark, *
    and evil lurks on every side,

PSALM 101: WHERE, THEN, AM I CALLED TO GO 183

11. Yet there is mercy freely given to those who ask, *
    who will call on the strength of the Lord.

12. The pilgrim seeks an enduring city, *
    and is never at home in this world.

13. Envy and flattery and falsehood are here, *
    pride and anger and violence on every side.

14. Those who go out of the way *
    are assailed by doubt and taken captive by despair.

15. But faith can overcome doubt, *
    and hope sets us free from despair.

16. One leak will sink a great ship, *
    and one sin can destroy one's life.

17. Those who forget their friends are unmerciful to their friends, *
    but those who forget their Savior are unmerciful to themselves.

18. The way of the transgressor is hard, *
    and the way of the slothful is a hedge of thorns.

19. Those who are humble need fear no fall, *
    but the proud are always in danger.

20. The pilgrim who would be valiant on the way,
    constant in any wind or weather, *
    must never relent or be discouraged;

21. Nor be frightened by wild beasts or giant adversaries, *
    nor discouraged by false stories;

22. For the pilgrim is determined to inherit the promise of life, *
    and therefore will not fear what others say.

23. So the pilgrim will cross over the river, *
    and all the trumpets will sound on the other side.

Psalm 102:
Tell Me, O Human Heart

Hugh of St. Victor (1096–1141)

1. Tell me, O human heart, what you would rather choose: *
    would you rejoice with the world
    or would you rejoice with God?

2. We choose the thing we love; *
    we love the one who loves us.

3. Through love we choose the road to follow; *
    through love we run the road we have chosen.

4. Through love we persevere in running the road; *
    through love we arrive at the journey's end.

5. Through love we grasp the object of our journey; *
    through love we enjoy the promised life of our native land.

6. Love is itself the road we follow; *
    love is also our leader on the way.

7. All roads come from love, *
    and all roads return to love.

8. Love is the perfection of the law, *
    and love is the fulfillment of truth.

9. Love is the road that brings God to the world; *
    love is the road by which we return to God.

10. Love draws God down to the depths of human life; *
    love draws us up, exalting us to the heights.

12. Love is the journey and the arrival; *
    love is our dwelling and blessedness.

13. Yet we are all too easily deceived; *
    we confuse love with pleasure.

14. We are easily contented to stay where we are, *
    and fail to see a greater treasure at the end of the road.

15. Come down to us, O Love of God, *
    enlighten our minds and enlarge our hearts.

16. Make room in our hearts, O Love of God, *
    live in us and give us life forever,

Psalm 103:
Listen to the Silence

Madeleine L'Engle (1918–2007)

1. Listen to the silence, *
    for it is in silence that the Word is spoken.

2. In silence the Word came to the womb of the God-bearer; *
    in silence the Word matures and comes to birth.

3. In silence the Word faces human authority and judgment; *
    in silence the Word awaits the third morning.

4. In silence the Word waits *
    for human hearts that are prepared to hear.

5. Come, now, Lord Jesus, *
    silence our noisiness.

6. Speak to the silent hearts, *
    that wait for your coming.

Psalm 104:
How Fragmentary Is Human Existence

Ladislaus Boros (1927–1981)

1. How fragmentary is human existence *
   and how fragile is human thought!

2. No shrewdness or calculation *
   can give knowledge of the meaning of life.

3. The meaning of life is present throughout the universe *
   in mystery beyond knowledge.

4. The answer to the mystery is a personal adventure *
   full of uncertainty and danger.

5. It is full of deep meaning, *
   but has no guaranteed security.

6. The effort to meet God in prayer *
   confronts us always with what is new and unexpected.

7. The answer found in prayer is not a possession, *
   but rather a knowing and a pilgrimage.

8. The questions take root and confront us with mystery: *
   where is God in my time of need?
   Why do I see such suffering?

9. The questions continue and upset our certainties; *
   our faith rocks and belief seems foolish.

10. Still the questions come as an inner necessity, *
    a compulsion like love which commands our life.

11. Doubt is essential to our prayer and our questioning; *
    in prayer we risks our own lives for answers.

12. Revelation is not a system but a destiny; *
    God shows us the way one step at a time.

Psalm 105:
Defend Me This Day

Lancelot Andrewes (1555–1626)

1. All glory is yours, Creator of life; *
    you separate light from darkness,
    and bring us again into light.

2. We praise you, O Lord, for the gift of sleep, *
    for rest after the work of the day
    and the renewal of our strength.

3. All glory is yours, Creator of light; *
    for the rays of the sun and the light of your Word;

4. For the writing of the Law, *
    and the vision of the prophets,

5. For apostles, missionaries, and martyrs *
    who have carried the light of your Word to all the world.

6. Open my eyes to see you in those I meet; *
    open my heart to respond to others
        in your Name and Spirit.

7. Defend me this day against all danger, *
    guide me in the decisions I make.

8. Show me the path to follow, *
    for I put my trust in you.

9. Teach me to do the work you have given me to do *
   to the glory of your name and the benefit of others.

10. Let the words I speak reflect your wisdom, *
    and let my actions reflect your love.

11. Guard me when I go out, *
    and be with me when I return.

12. Let me come to the end of the day in thankfulness *
    for all things are your gift.

Psalm 106:
The Only Way to Express Our Love

Dorothy Day (1897–1980)

1. The only way to express our love for God *
   is to love our brothers and sisters in need.

2. Love of our brothers and sisters means voluntary poverty; *
   it involves putting aside our natural instincts for comfort.

3. When our brothers and sisters suffer, *
   we must suffer with them.

4. When our brothers and sisters lack necessities, *
   we cannot enjoy our comforts.

5. We are called to be perfect as God is perfect, *
   and we must always aim at perfection
   even though we fall short.

6. We must keep this vision in mind and accept its truth, *
   even when we cannot live up to it.

7. Poverty means avoiding food and clothing made
   by exploiting others; *
   poverty means simplicity of life
   following the example of the saints.

8. How far we are from the life to which we are called! *
   How blind we are to our weaknesses!

9. Common sense persuades us that we can live well and be generous, *
    that we can be comfortable ourselves and still care for others.

10. The candlelight of common sense shows us an easier way, *
    but the flaming sun of justice reveals the truth.

11. We may have more time with modern conveniences, *
    but we will not have more love.

12. Let us lavish gifts on others as God lavishes gifts on us; *
    let us rejoice in poverty as Christ became poor for us.

13. We must believe in poverty for love of Christ and love of the poor; *
    we cannot love those we do not know,
    or know those we seldom see.

14. No matter what happens to us, *
    it is possible always to praise God.

15. We are called to love with understanding *
    and to love without understanding.

16. We are called to love blindly; *
    we are called to see only what is loveable.

17. We are called to see only the best in others, *
    to see their virtues and not their faults.

18. We are called to see Christ in others, *
    and to find Christ in ourselves.

Psalm 107:
O Love, Beyond All Knowing

John Baillie (1886–1960)

1. O Love, beyond all knowing, *
    O Love, forever seeking human hearts,

2. Give me grace to throw open the door of my heart; *
    let your light and love flow in.

3. Give me open ears, Lord God, *
    to hear your voice calling me to serve.

4. Give me courage to answer, Here am I; *
    let me hear your voice in the voices of my sisters and brothers,
    and when I hear, respond to their needs.

5. Give me an open mind, O Lord, *
    to receive and to welcome new light on my road.

6. Give me courage to change my mind when that is needed, *
    and open my mind and heart to the light
    that may come to me from others.

7. Give me open eyes to see you in the world you have made, *
    let the things you have made fill me with joy,
    and let them lift my mind to you their Creator.

8. Forgive me my blindness to human need, *
    help me to see you in the hungry and homeless and suffering.

9. Give me open hands, Lord God, *
    to share with others what you have given me.

10. Let me hold as a steward all you have given me, *
    and make my life an offering of praise.

Psalm 108:
God Has Plans for a Future of Peace

Brother Roger of Taizé (1915–2005)

1. God has plans for a future of peace for us; *
    God wants to give us a future and a hope.

2. The world is longing for a future of peace, *
    to be freed from threats of violence.

3. We must not let ourselves be caught up in a spiral of gloom; *
    God did not create us to be subject to a blind destiny.

4. Let us then prepare for a future of peace and not of misfortune; *
    let us make our lives a light that shines for others.

5. Let us be bearers of peace and trust
    in situations of crisis and conflict; *
    let us move on even when trials or failures weigh us down.

6. The first essential of peace is a simple trust in God, *
    a renewed commitment undertaken countless times in the course of our life.

7. Doubts will come but they must never disturb us; *
    the Holy Spirit remains with us always.

8. Happy those who seek for simplicity, *
    simplicity of heart and simplicity of life.

9. The simple heart attempts to live in the present moment, *
    to welcome each day as God's gift.

10. A simple heart does not claim to understand everything about faith on its own; *
   the spirit of simplicity shines out in serene joy and cheerfulness.

11. Simplifying our life enables us to share with the least fortunate, *
   to alleviate suffering where there is disease and poverty and famine.

12. Many words are not needed in order to pray; *
   a few words are enough to entrust everything to God, our fears as well as our hopes.

13. The Holy Spirit kindles a glimmer of light within us; *
   it awakens in our hearts the desire for God.

14. The simple desire for God is already an act of prayer; *
   nothing is more responsible than to pray.

15. The more we make our own a prayer which is simple and humble, *
   the more we are led to love and to express it with our life.

16. The Church does not exist for itself but for the world, *
   to place within it a ferment of peace.

17. In God's presence fear and worry are driven out; *
   all God can do is love us.

18. In prayer we know that we are never alone: *
   the Holy Spirit sustains in us a communion with God, and leads us on into the life which has no end.

Psalm 109:
Blessed Are You, O Lord

Elisabeth Leseur (1866–1914)

1. Blessed are you, O Lord my God, for the sufferings I endure *
    that draw me near to your heart.

2. I belong to you and hope always to belong to you, *
    in suffering or joy, in illness or health, in life or in death.

3. I seek and desire to seek only one end: *
    to promote your glory by accomplishing your desires for me.

4. I offer myself to you in whole-hearted sacrifice *
    and ask that you use me in your service
    on behalf of those whom you love.

5. Let me always be strict with myself *
    but gentle, loving, and helpful to others.

6. When I feel powerless against hostility and indifference, *
    teach me to turn to offer my prayers and quiet example.

7. Teach me to be silent about myself, *
    but generous in praise for others.

8. May your kingdom come in those who are dear to me; *
    may your kingdom be fully established in me.

9. Make me your instrument and use me, my Lord, *
    for the good of all others and for your greater glory.

10. I offer you, my Lord, the sadness, disappointments
    and injuries of my heart, *
        the anxieties and sufferings of this life.

11. I offer you darkness of spirit, weakness of will, *
        I offer you interior sorrows and burdens.

12. I offer you my physical distress and limitations, *
        the discomforts and exhaustion that trouble me now.

13. I bind all these in a sheaf, Lord God; *
        I come humbly with the shepherds
        to lay them in the manger.

14. Holy Child, all love and simplicity, *
        accept my afflictions and use them for the good of others
        and for your glory.

15. May your holy hands help me to carry my burdens, *
        may your love relieve my isolation.

16. Teach me, O God, a stronger and deeper love *
        and use me for the spreading of your kingdom.

Psalm 110:
If You Would Be a Servant of God

Abba Philemon (7th Century)

1. If you would be a servant of God, *
    flee from all that draws you to this world
    and follow the path of the saints.

2. Dress simply; behave simply; speak calmly; *
    walk humbly; turn away from wealth;
    let yourself be despised.

3. Lay claim to no city or home or possessions; *
    free yourself from all concerns of this world.

4. Be compassionate, gentle, quiet; *
    prepare your heart to be marked as God's own.

5. The heart is like wax that can be marked; *
    erase the letters written on your heart
    so that God can write on it.

6. The servants of God are those who observe God's laws *
    and therefore shine like lights in the world,

7. Through self-control and love for God, *
    they are radiant with holy words and deeds.

8. Through constant prayer and study of God's Word, *
    they open their spiritual eyes to see the Creator of all things.

9. Great joy and fierce longing burn within them, *
    they belong to the heavenly realm.

Psalm 111:
Learn to Let Go of God

Anonymous (7th Century)

1. Learn to let go of God; *
    there is no power that can take God from you.

2. If you desire to eat of the honey, *
    do not be put off by the sting of the bee.

3. Though you see the heavens torn apart and the stars begin to fall, *
    no created thing can separate you from God.

4. Listen and look and be still; *
    let the light fill your inmost being.

5. Never complain; always be patient; *
    God remains present in the depths of your heart.

6. O deep treasure, how will you be dug up? *
    O highest perfection, who can come into your presence?

7. O flowing fountain of water, who can drain your abundance? *
    O burning light, O radiance of love, who can resist
    your transforming power?

8. O silent outcry, speaking to all in every created thing, *
    no one can find you who will not let you go.

Psalm 112:
My Heart Has No Rest

Nicholas of Cusa (1401–1464)

1. My heart has no rest, O Lord, *
    because you have filled it with a great desire
    that you alone can satisfy.

2. I experience your goodness, Lord God, *
    which feeds me with a growing desire.

3. Blessed are you, Lord God, who nourish me first with milk *
    and lead me on to more solid food.

4. When I see you, Lord God, in Paradise, *
    I see that you are beyond all that can be said or thought.

5. You, O God, cannot be seen by human beings, *
    yet you can be seen in all that you have created.

6. Draw me to yourself, for I cannot come unless you draw me, *
    set me free from this world and united to you
    in an eternity of glorious life.

7. O fountain of riches, who wills to be held in my possession, *
    the treasury of joy that no one can desire to end;

8. O height of riches, beyond all understanding, *
    to you be praise and glory through endless ages. Amen.

Psalm 113:
Varied, Indeed, and Marvelous

John of Forde (1145–1214)

1. Varied, indeed, and marvelous, *
    is the love of God for God's people.

2. God's love is a river of peace, *
    streaming out and flowing gently.

3. God's love is also a torrent *
    that sweeps everything before it.

4. What response can we make to this overwhelming love? *
    We look up in wonder at the majesty of God's love;
    we gaze within at the marvel of its goodness.

5. God's love flows out freely from the abundance of its source; *
    it pours out with force and insists on its way.

6. The treasure of our love is hidden in the field of our heart; *
    it lies buried in the depths of our being.

7. With great effort we can dig up a little of this love, *
    but it is earthy and impure.

8. If our love is to be of use and value, it must be purified: *
    it needs to be smelted in a blazing fire.

9. Who can describe, who can even gaze at,
   the brightness of God's love? *
   > It moves from brightness to brightness,
   > and light is seen in light.

10. The love of the church is a light and a flaming fire, *
    > but the burning and shining come from the love of God.

11. Eternally it draws from God's love and eternally pours it back; *
    > it can never grow dim or faint.

12. How ancient, sublime, generous, and spontaneous, *
    > how precious, how weighty, how firm,
    > how radiant is love.

13. May God, the font of all love, *
    > bless us gloriously with that love.

14. May we be blessed through Jesus Christ, the only Son of God's love, *
    > who lives and who reigns for ever.

Psalm 114:
I Know That the Almighty God Is Present

Jeremy Taylor (1613–1667)

1. I know that the Almighty God is present in every place, *
    God sees every act, hears every word,
    understands every thought.

2. I know that God is present in every place, *
    but not restricted to any place.

3. We can no more be removed from the presence of God *
    than we can be separated from our own selves.

4. The stars and the planets are held in God's hand, *
    the constellations are shaped by God's fingers,

5. God's eye guides every living creature; *
    God's breath refreshes them.

6. The fish of the sea, the birds of the air,
    the wild animals of the wilderness, *
    all are given life by the Lord God.

7. The glory of God is revealed in the holy places; *
    and made known in the lives of God's chosen people.

8. God is present among the homeless and hungry, *
    God strengthens the persecuted and oppressed.

9. God dwells in our hearts by faith, *
    and the reign of God is established among us.

Psalm 115:
Peace Is the Highest Good

Desiderius Erasmus (1466–1536)

1. Peace is the highest good; *
    let all who love life pursue it.

2. But do not seek the false peace promised by the world; *
    seek the peace of Christ which the world cannot give.

3. There is but one way to peace; *
    we must wage war with ourselves.

4. We must wage a fierce war with our faults; *
    these separate us from God.

5. Christ is the author of wisdom, *
    and he is wisdom himself.

6. Christ is the true light, *
    the splendor of eternal glory.

7. Through the wisdom of Christ and his example, *
    the malice of the enemy is overcome.

8. If we seek the wisdom of Christ, *
    in Christ we shall also conquer.

9. Embrace the wisdom of Christ, *
    and reject the wisdom of the world.

10. There is no greater foolishness than worldly wisdom, *
    those who are wise will reject it.

11. What wisdom is it that is skillful in useless things? *
    It should be pitied rather than followed.

12. Seek the wisdom of God with all your strength, *
    dig it out of the Scriptures like gold from the mine.

13. The crown of God-given wisdom is to know yourself, *
    but all wisdom must agree with the Scriptures.

14. Our battle is not with human opponents, *
    but a struggle within ourselves.

15. Assume the life of Christ as your goal, *
    and pursue it with all the grace that God supplies.

16. Do all that you can to save your life, *
    to escape eternal death.

17. Since faith is the only gateway to Christ, *
    rely first of all on the Scriptures.

18. Be sure there is nothing so true, *
    as the words to be found in the Scriptures.

Psalm 116:
We Look for the World

Francis Thompson (1859–1907)

1. We look for the world that cannot be seen *
    and reach for the world that cannot be touched.

2. We seek to understand the world beyond human knowledge *
    and grasp the world that human hands cannot hold.

3. The fish swims in the ocean and the eagle soars through the air *
    yet we feel estranged from the world we inhabit.

4. We search the swirling galaxies for understanding *
    and ignore the presence at our own door.

5. The invisible powers remain present throughout creation; *
    touch a leaf, feel the sun's warmth, and the unity is there.

6. It is we who are estranged from the Creator *
    and blind to the many-splendored thing.

7. Yet in our darkest night Jacob's ladder is present, *
    set up between heaven and Times Square.

8. Yes, in that dark night of the soul, cry out *
    and there is Christ walking on the water,
    not of Galilee but here, coming to us where we are.

Psalm 117:
We Come to You This Morning

James Weldon Johnson (1871–1938)

1. We come to you ths morning, Lord God, *
   with our knees bowed down and our bodies bent in prayer.

2. We come to the throne of grace, Lord God, *
   from the lonesome valley of our lives.

3. O Lord our God, we come to you this day, *
   like empty pitchers to an ever-flowing fountain.

4. We come to you, O Lord our God, *
   with no right to enter your presence
   and no gifts to offer.

5. Open the window of heaven we pray, *
   and lean far out over our troubled earth
   and listen to our prayers.

6. Have mercy, Lord, have mercy, *
   hear our prayers and have mercy.

7. And now, O Lord, as I go about my day, *
   hold me in the hollow of your hand.

8. Wash me through and through from my sins, *
   give me a clean heart and mind.

9. Let your word strike me like hammer blows, *
   and break down the walls I build against you.

10. Open my eyes to see beyond the narrow streets I travel, *
    let me see the straight way to your kingdom
    and give me strength to follow it.

Psalm 118:
By the Way of the Shepherds

Theodore Parker Ferris (1908–1972)

1. By the way of the shepherds of Bethlehem, *
    lead us, O Lord, to find newness of life.

2. By the innocence of the Christ Child, *
    renew our simple trust.

3. By the tenderness of Mary, *
    deliver us from cruelty and hardness of heart.

4. By the patience of Joseph, *
    save us from all rash judgment and action.

5. By the watchfulness of the shepherds, *
    open our eyes to the signs of your coming.

6. By the journey of the wise men, *
    keep our searching spirits from despair.

7. By the music of the angels' choir, *
    silence in us the clamor of the world.

8. By the shining of a star, *
    guide our feet in the way of peace.

Psalm 119:
Use Me Then

William Barclay (1907–1978)

1. Use me then, my Savior, *
    for any purpose and in any way,
    wherever the need may be.

2. Here is my heart, an empty vessel: *
    fill it with your gifts of grace.

3. Here is my troubled soul: *
    quicken it and refresh it with your love.

4. Take my voice and use it, *
    to spread abroad your Name.

5. Use the gifts you have given me, *
    for the building up of your church.

6. Never, Lord, I pray, let my trust in you waver; *
    always, Lord, let your Name be glorified.

Psalm 120:
Thanks Be to You

Catherine of Siena (1347–1380)

1. Thanks be to you, eternal God, for not rejecting me
   your handiwork, *
   > nor turning your face from me,
   > nor making light of my desires.

2. In your light you have given me light; *
   > in your wisdom I have found the truth,
   > in your mercy I have found your love for my neighbors.

3. Why do you come to me, Lord God? *
   > Not for my virtues, but only because of your mercy.

4. Let this same love enlighten my understanding
   with the light of faith, *
   > let me know your truth as you reveal it to me.

5. Let my memory be strong enough to recall your mercy; *
   > let my will be set ablaze in your charity's fire.

6. Let that fire burst forth in my flesh and my blood; *
   > grant me the key of obedience to open heaven's gate.

7. O eternal Trinity! O everliving Godhead! *
   > You are a deep and endless sea!

8. The more I enter you, the more I discover; *
   > the more I discover, the more I seek to know.

9. In you the soul is satisfied yet remains always hungry; *
    always the soul thirsts for you,
    always the soul longs for more light.

10. How long will you hide your face from my eyes? *
    When shall I see you in truth?

11. Eternal Trinity, fire and abyss of love, *
    raise me up to know you in truth!
    Let me live to praise and glorify your Name!

12. By the light of understanding,
    I have seen the beauty of your creation; *
    I have tasted your depth, O eternal Trinity.

13. When I see myself in your light, *
    I see that I am made in your image.

14. You have gifted me with power from yourself, Eternal God; *
    you have filled me with your understanding and wisdom.

15. You, eternal Trinity, are the craftsman and I am your handiwork; *
    you have shown me your love for your creation.

16. O deepest abyss! O eternal Godhead! O everflowing sea! *
    What more could you give me than the gift of yourself?

Psalm 121:
I Praise, Adore, and Worship

Leslie Weatherhead (1893–1976)

1. I praise, adore, and worship you, O God, *
    for all the splendors shown to me,
    at which I gaze in awe.

2. You are the ultimate Artist and Creator of the beauty *
    before which I stand in awe.

2. Yet I also am artist and creator; *
    therefore I love your work.

3. I praise you for the strong mountains that so lift my spirits, *
    and for the wooded glades that enfold me like a great cathedral.

4. I praise you for the soaring mountain range *
    that lifts my spirits with its power,

5. I thank you for the breathtaking splendor of sunsets, *
    and the long, quiet afterglow that silhouettes the mountains
    against the evening sky.

6. I thank you for those dawns that reflect the eternal joy
    at the heart of things, *
    and the loneliness of the far stretching moors.

7. I thank you for the rush of the mountain streams
    and the laughing waters, *
    for the bluebell glens and the shy fish in secret pools.

8. I thank you for the power of waves crashing on rocks, *
    and for the spray flung high in the air.

9. I thank you for the quiet and solemn majesty of the stars, *
    and for the hunger to understand that the night sky evokes.

10. I thank you for the cluster of primroses
    in the cleft of the lichen-covered rocks, *
        and for the trill of a lark mounting higher
        into the trackless blue.

11. I thank you for the bleating of sheep on the hillside above the valley *
    and the crunch of cows' hooves in the frozen mud
    in the farmyard gateway.

12. I thank you for rooks at eveningtide tumbling into their nests
    in an old elm, *
        and for a field of buttercups on a spring morning,
        and for a flowering chestnut tree in June.

13. I thank you for a moonlit river flowing quietly
    through a silent night, *
        and for the gentle rustle of silver leaves in midnight trees.

14. O God of beauty, in whose world I hear the echoes of your voice *
    and see the traces of your hand,

15. As you have enabled me to catch these faint echoes
    of your presence, *
        accept my tribute of praise.

Psalm 122:
The Land Is So Beautiful

Oscar Romero (1917–1980)

1. The land is so beautiful, the fields and the farms, *
    but we see it groan under oppression and abuse,
    and the church feels the pain.

2. Nature looks for a liberation, *
    to be freed from sinful hands
    and rejoice in God the Liberator.

3. Preaching that does not point out sin, *
    is not the preaching of the gospel.

4. Preaching that makes sinners feel good, *
    betrays the gospel's call.

5. Preaching that awakens us, as when a light is turned on, *
    upsets the sleeper, the sinner,
    but that is the message we proclaim.

6. The church cannot be deaf to the millions *
    who cry out for liberation from a thousand oppressions.

7. The church proclaims the true liberty, *
    which is freedom first of all from sin.

8. Those who put their faith in the Risen one, *
    those who cry out against oppression,

9. Those who begin their struggle with the Risen One, *
    they alone are true followers of Christ.

10. We must not be led astray by the allure of power and money; *
    true hope is not found in violence and bloodshed;

11. True hope is found in Christ who reigns after death, *
    and with him reign all who seek his justice,
    his hope, and his peace.

12. Let us sing a song of hope and be filled with a spirit of joy, *
    knowing that Christ becomes flesh in the faithful.

13. Let us have faith that the evil will pass away *
    and we shall awake to the Lord's great feast.

14. All those who struggle for justice, *
    are working for the kingdom of God.

15. If the skies have darkened on our human history, *
    let us not lose hope.

16. Let us hope for the hour of liberation; *
    that hour will come because God is faithful.

Psalm 123:
Come, for the Fields Are White

Evelyn Underhill (1875–1941)

1. Come, for the fields are white to harvest: *
    come and see the timeless mystery of love.

2. Come, see how it is that we feed on God, *
    see the One who is our bread indeed.

3. Torn by the sickles, see him share the travail of Creation: *
    see him maimed and despised,

4. Yet he remains the more dearly prized by those who love him, *
    because he lays his beauty down for us.

5. Trace here on these fields his everlasting Cross, *
    and over the stricken sheaves see the Immortal Victim's crown.

6. From far horizons came a Voice that said, *
    "Take now your daily bread from the hand of Death."

7. Then awakening, I saw revealed *
    a splendor burning in the heart of things:

8. I saw the flame of living love which lights the law *
    of mystic death that works the mystic birth.

9. I knew the patient passion of the earth, *
    maternal, everlasting, from which springs
    the Bread of Angels and the life of man.

10. Now in each blade I am too blind to see *
    the glory of God's growth:

11. Yet in my blindness still I know *
    a foretaste of the Immemorial Plan.

12. Here I have understood *
    how all things are one great oblation:

13. He is on our altars, *
    we are on the world's cross.

14. Like this earth-born grain *
    we are snatched from the sod;

15. We, too, are reaped and ground to grist, *
    crushed and tormented in the mills of God,
    and offered as a living Eucharist.

Psalm 124:
Who Is There Who Truly Loves

John Chrysostom (347–407)

1. Who is there who truly loves God? *
    Let them come to the Lord's own feast!

2. Who are there who are grateful servants? *
    Let them rejoice in the joy of their Lord!

3. Are there any who are weary with fasting? *
    Let them come to receive their wages!

4. If any have toiled from the first hour, *
    let them come to receive their reward;

5. If any have come after the third hour, *
    let them with gratitude join in the Feast!

6. And those that arrived after the sixth hour, *
    let him not doubt that they, too, will be rewarded.

7. If any delayed until the ninth hour to come, *
    let them not hesitate; but let them come too.

8. And those who arrived only at the eleventh hour, *
    let them not be afraid by reason of their delay.

9. For the Lord is gracious and receives the last even as the first; *
    our God gives rest to those who come
    even at the eleventh hour,

10. To this one God gives, and to another God bestows, *
    God accepts the works as God greets the endeavor.

11. God honors the deed and commends the intention; *
    let us all enter into the joy of the Lord!

12. First and last alike receive your reward; *
    rich and poor, rejoice together!

13. You that have kept the fast, and you that have not, *
    rejoice today for the Table is richly laden!

14. Feast royally at the Lord's Table; *
    let no one go away hungry.

15. Partake, one and all, of the cup of faith. *
    enjoy all the riches of God's goodness!

16. Let none grieve at their poverty, *
    for the universal kingdom has been revealed.

17. Let none mourn that they have fallen again and again; *
    for forgiveness has risen from the grave.

18. Let no one fear death, for the death of our Savior has set us free. *
    he has destroyed it by enduring it.

19. Hell was in an uproar because it was done away with; *
    Hell was in an uproar because it is mocked.

20. Hell came to earth, and encountered Heaven; *
    it took what it saw, and was overcome by what it did not see.

21. Christ is Risen, and you, O death, are annihilated! *
    Christ is Risen, and the evil ones are cast down!

22. Christ is Risen, and the angels rejoice! *
    Christ is Risen, and life has been set free!

Psalm 125:
Listen to My Voice

Columbanus (543–615)

1. Listen to my voice and hear the word of life; *
   quench your soul's thirst with the water of life.

2. Drink but do not fully quench your thirst; *
   drink and never be satisfied for there is always more to receive.

3. The fountain of life calls to us,
   the fountain of love summons us, *
   "All those who thirst, let them come to me and drink."

4. The Lord Christ is the fountain of life; *
   he invites us to the fountain that we may drink and be revived.

5. Whoever loves God drinks of this water; *
   you who are filled with the Word of God, come and drink.

6. Drink and never be satisfied; *
   drink and never be filled.

7. If you are thirsty, drink of the water of life, *
   if you are hungry, eat of the bread of life.

8. Blessed are those who drink of this fountain, *
   blessed are those who eat of this bread.

9. The author of life is the fountain of life; *
   the creator of light is the source of illumination.

10. The Lord is the fountain of living water: *
    the water is the drink of eternal life.

11. Christ is the fountain of life and of light; *
    wisdom and light and life come from him.

12. You, O God, are the fountain ever to be desired, *
    the fountain that never fails,
    that wells up to eternal life.

Psalm 126:
Why Are the Changes

Boethius (475–524)

1. Why are the changes of Nature bound in place *
    by a fixed and ordered round?

2. What power is it that bends toward peace *
    the warring elements of nature?

3. What is the power that holds in place the restless seas, *
    keeping them within their appointed boundaries?

4. It is love that holds the chains, *
    love that reigns over the sea and the earth.

5. Love—whom else but sovereign Love? *
    Love is lord in the highest heaven!

6. But if Love should fail to take such care, *
    all that is now so closely knit together
    in the bonds of love and holy peace,

7. Would fall into conflict and strife *
    and shake all the fabric of the world.

8. Tribes and nations are united by Love, *
    by just treaties and impartial agreements.

9. The bonds of marriage also are sanctified by Love; *
    Love appoints faithful patterns to true friendship.

10. Love, all-sovereign Love, provides such gifts; *
    blessed are we if the love that rules the sky
    is enthroned as well in our hearts.

Psalm 127:
Look Down, O God

Martin Luther (1483–1546)

1. Look down, O God, from heaven and see *
    how few are your servants,
    how helpless are those who love you.

2. Your Word is everywhere rejected, *
    and Faith is overwhelmed by doubt.

3. Trouble and distress surround us; *
    the times are dark and full of fear.

4. We see false teaching spread abroad, *
    human doctrines not based on your Word.

5. Divisions increase among us; *
    we long for unity but cannot find it.

6. Outwardly, what is taught seems reasonable, *
    but one goes here and another goes there
    and the Church is torn apart.

7. Now therefore God says, "I will rise up, *
    I will come to my people and give them help.

8. "I have heard the bitter complaint of my people, *
    and I will grant their request.

9. "I will send out my Word in battle; *
    I will defend the poor and conquer those who do wrong."

10. As silver is purified by fire, *
    so shall God's Word shine forth at last.

11. Through many trials we shall learn its power, *
    and all shall see how great is its glory.

12. Preserve your Word, O God, in purity *
    and make it secure in our hearts.

Psalm 128:
God Sees Us

Martin Luther (1483–1546)

1. God sees us in our poverty and weakness, *
    and knows we have nothing to offer.

2. God's love flows from the heart of God, *
    the wellspring of all that is good.

3. The heart of the giver makes the gift precious, *
    for it comes from a hand we love.

4. God is nothing else but pure, unspeakable love, *
    greater and more than we can think or imagine.

5. Though we fail to notice or give thanks to God, *
    still the sun shines and the grass grows.

6. God pours forth for us not only sun and moon, heaven and earth, *
    but God gives us the Son of God to live and die for us.

7. How then can we doubt or be uncertain *
    that God is merciful, gracious, patient, faithful, and true.

8. God is not only faithful and patient, merciful, gracious, and true; *
    but has done already far more than was promised.

9. God reconciles us to the heart of God *
    and is favorable and heartily gracious to us;
    God's nature is all pure love.

11. What is the reason God gives? What moves God to love us? *
    It is nothing but love, for God delights to give and to bless.

12. What does God give? Not empires only, *
    not a world of silver and gold, not heaven and earth,

13. God's gift is as great as the eternal and unknowable God; *
    a gift as infinite as the giver.

14. God's gift to us is the spring and fountain of all grace, *
    the possession of all the riches and treasures of God.

Psalm 129:
You, O God, Are from Everlasting

Miles Lowell Yates (1890–1956)

1. You, O God, are from everlasting to everlasting; *
    your truth endures for ever.

2. You are the source of all things; *
    you sustain the worlds in their order
    and hold our souls in life.

3. You are wisdom and power and love; *
    in your sure hands are all the issues of existence.

4. You are the all-holy one who hate evil, *
    in whose sight all evil must be judged.

5. You are the all-merciful one who knows our weakness, *
    whose every judgment is right.

6. Out of my doubts and fears I come to acknowledge you; *
    out of my forgetfulness I come to remember you.

7. Out of my pride I come with humility; *
    out of my sin I come with repentance.

8. Out of my discouragement I come with trust; *
    out of my darkness I come to your light.

9. Out of my weakness I come to your strength; *
    out of my restlessness I come to your peace.

Psalm 130:
Lord, Increase My Faith

George Appleton (1902–1993)

1. Lord, increase my faith *
    that I may embrace your will.

2. Lord, increase my faith, *
    and help me to overcome obstacles in my path.

3. Lord, increase my faith, *
    and help me find ways to serve you.

4. Lord, increase my faith, *
    and decrease my impatience and frustration.

5. Lord, increase my faith, *
    and teach me always to turn to you in my need.

6. Lord, increase my faith, *
    that I may see you with the eyes of faith.

7. Lord, fill me with faith and hope and love, *
    this day and forever.

Psalm 131:
Take, Lord, and Receive

Ignatius of Loyola (1491–1556)

1. Take, Lord, and receive all my liberty as a gift; *
    I give you my memory, my understanding, and my will:
    all that I have and call my own.

2. You, O Lord, have given everything to me; *
    to you, O Lord, I return all that you have given me.

3. All that I have is yours; do with it what you will; *
    give me only your love and your grace,
    and that will be enough.

4. Lord, teach me to be generous; *
    teach me to serve you as you deserve.

5. Teach me to give and not to count the cost; *
    teach me to toil and not to seek for rest.

6. Teach me to labor and not to ask for reward, *
    save that of knowing that I do your will.

Psalm 132:
We Are to Be Like a City

John Winthrop, Thomas Jefferson, Abraham Lincoln, Franklin D. Roosevelt, Martin Luther King, Jr.

1. We are to be like a city set on a hill, *
    whose failure and victories will be visible to the whole world.

2. So that if we shall deal falsely with our God
    in this work we have undertaken, *
    we shall be consumed out of the good land we have been given.

3. Therefore let us choose life, that we and our children may live, *
    by obeying God's voice and uniting ourselves with the Lord
    who is our life and our prosperity.

4. We are a community blessed with abundance *
    and called to be stewards of God's gifts.

5. We hold this truth to be self-evident: *
    that all human beings are created with equal rights,
    the right to life and freedom and opportunity.

6. Drawn to the nation that upholds these truths,
    some came out of oppression to seek freedom, *
    others came in chains
    and yearned also for freedom.

7. Out of the farms and plantations,
    the tenements of the cities, and the strife of the battlefield, *
    the gift of freedom has been renewed and expanded.

8. Challenged often by tyrants, attacked by destroyers, *
   brave men and women have shed their blood
   to defend and extend the gift of freedom.

9. Constantly we must rededicate ourselves to the cause *
   for which others gave the last full measure of devotion.

10. Still we hold up the dream of a new birth of freedom, *
    freedom at last for those of every race and gender,

11. Freedom from fear and hunger and insecurity, *
    freedom to pursue the dream of a renewed humanity,

12. Freedom to realize the potential that lies within us *
    and to create the promised community
    of justice, freedom, and peace.

13. We must therefore hold each other in close affection; *
    we must be willing to sacrifice our own convenience
    to supply the needs of others.

14. We must work together in all patience and mutual concern; *
    we must delight in each other and make other's
    conditions our own.

15. We must rejoice together, mourn together,
    labor and suffer together, *
       always holding before our eyes our community in the work,
       as members of the same body.

16. So shall we keep the unity of the spirit in the bond of peace; *
    then the Lord will be our God, and delight to dwell among us.

17. With malice toward none, with charity for all, *
    with firmness in the right as God gives us to see the right,
    let us strive on toward the vision we are given.

18. Let us seek constantly to heal the divisions among us, *
    to work together toward a just and lasting peace
    among ourselves and with all nations.

Psalm 133:
When Your Church Awakens

William Barclay (1907–1978)

1. When your church awakens to the gospel, O Lord, *
    then will your Name be made known in all the world;

2. Then will the nations sing for joy *
    and come together in peace.

3. When your church awakens to justice, O Lord, *
    then will bodies be redeemed as well as souls;

4. Then will those who work be rewarded fairly, *
    and those who cannot work will be secure.

5. When your church awakens to adventure, O Lord, *
    then will worship be offered with understanding;

6. Then will children come together with singing, *
    and young people find new ways to serve.

7. When your church awakens to the Holy Spirit, Lord, *
    then will your people be united
    across all barriers of race and clan.

8. Then will we be gathered together in fellowship, *
    across all divisions of social difference;

9. When your church truly knows itself to be the Body of Christ, *
    then will the hungry be fed and the sick find healing, *

PSALM 133: WHEN YOUR CHURCH AWAKENS

10. Then will the young find effective guidance, *
    and the elderly find the support they need,

11. Then will the lonely find fellowship, *
    and the tempted gain strength to choose rightly,

12. Then will the doubting find answers, *
    and the sinners find forgiveness.

13. When your church awakens to hear good news, O Lord, *
    then will the world also know your love.

14. Then will peace flow down like a river, *
    and justice like a mighty stream.

Psalm 134:
I Turn to You

Harriet Beecher Stowe (1811–1896)

1. I turn to you when purple morning breaks, *
    when birds awake and night's dark shadows flee;

2. But fairer than the morning and the daylight *
    is my awareness that I am with you.

3. I am with you in times of darkness; *
    I am with you when nature is reborn;

4. I am with you in quiet adoration *
    in the calm quiet of the morning.

5. As in the dawn when the western star rests quietly on the ocean, *
    so in this dawning, I rest quietly on you.

6. In this quietness and new dawn, *
    may you find your image deep within me.

7. Still may I be with you so that each new-born morning *
    may be given a fresh and solemn splendor;

8. So may each new day awaken consciousness *
    that I am near you and your realm of life.

9. So also when evening comes and darkness falls, *
    I turn to you again in quiet prayer;

10. My rest is peaceful as I know your overshadowing protection, *
    but greater peace comes when I awake and find you present.

11. So may it be at last in a final morning *
    when life's shadows end and I awaken to light.

12. Then, when a brighter light than this earth's sun shines on me, *
    may I know forever that I am with you.

Psalm 135:
Our God, My God

Desmond Tutu (1931–)

1. Our God, my God, why have you forsaken us? *
    My God, our God, when will we ever learn?

2. When will we ever learn that you intended us for Shalom, *
    that you created us for wholeness and peace?

3. When will we learn that you created us for fellowship, *
    that you meant us for togetherness, for family?

4. When will we learn that you created us as your children, *
    that you intended us to be members of one family?

5. God, my Father and Mother,
    I am filled with anguish and puzzlement; *
        why, oh God, is there so much suffering,
        such needless suffering?

6. Everywhere we look there is pain and suffering; *
        why must there be so much killing,
        so much death and destruction?

7. Why is there so much bloodshed and so much suffering? *
        Why is there so much oppression, and injustice, and poverty
        and hunger?

8. Why, oh why, my God, our God, my Father, our Mother, *
        why must your people endure all the mindless violence?

PSALM 135: OUR GOD, MY GOD

9. Oh God, my God, our God, is there some explanation? *
    Can you explain why your people must suffer
    even in the land of the Prince of Peace?

10. I don't understand, oh God, my God, *
    why must there be so much pain and suffering
    in your creation, so very good and beautiful?

11. I am dumbfounded, *
    I am bewildered and in agony.

12. This is the world you loved so much
    that you gave your only begotten Son, *
    to hang from the cross to die.

13. Love was nearly overwhelmed by hate, *
    light was nearly extinguished by darkness.

14. But love has vanquished hate; *
    there life overcame death.

15. There on the cross light overwhelmed darkness, *
    therefore we can live with hope.

16. Yet there is carnage here and devastation there; *
    what are we to make of it all?

17. All I know, God, is that it's all so horrendous; *
    that we are so advanced that we can bomb with precision
    and people die and blood flows.

18. In the Eucharist as we offer the bread, *
    that bread contains all the bewilderment,
    the anguish, the blood, and the pain;

19. That bread contains the injustice; *
    it contains the poverty, hate and anger, fear and death;

20. In this bread we offer it all together, *
    we offer the perfect all-sufficient sacrifice
    of the Lamb without blemish.

21. We offer the bread for peace, for transfiguration, for compassion, *
    for soldiers and civilians, for family, for human togetherness.

22. Oh my God, our God, when will they ever learn? *
    When will we ever learn?

Psalm 136:
When I Wake to a New Day

Eric Milner-White (1884–1963)

1. When I wake to a new day *
   let me awake to your presence.

2. Let my earthly walk waken into song *
   and let my spirit rejoice in your presence.

3. Each new day is filled with wonder; *
   each new day is a gift from your hand.

4. Let me find you in all things around me; *
   be the light of each day and my endless day.

5. It is your light that touches all creation around me; *
   it is in your light that I see light.

6. In the light of your glory let me take up my work; *
   in the light of your glory let me offer my day to you.

7. This day may bring challenges; *
   let me meet them in faithfulness.

8. This day may bring opportunities; *
   let me offer them to your glory.

Psalm 137:
Happy Is She Who Is Called

Clare of Assisi (1194–1253)

1. Happy is she who is called to the banquet of life; *
    she may cling to him whose beauty awes the hosts of heaven.

2. She is called to the One whose love inspires love, *
    whose contemplation refreshes, whose generosity satisfies,
    whose memory shines like the dawn.

3. She is called to the one whose fragrance revives the dead, *
    whose vision blesses the citizens of the heavenly Jerusalem,

4. The splendor of eternal glory,
    the brightness of eternal light, *
        the mirror without a cloud.

5. You who are called to be married to Christ, *
    look into that mirror and study well your reflection,

6. Adorn yourself with a garment of every virtue; *
    deck yourself with holy poverty, humility,
    and love beyond words.

7. Behold the birth of this mirror, *
    laid in a manger, clothed in bands of cloth.

8. What wondrous humility! What marvelous poverty! *
    The Lord of heaven and earth, resting in a manger.

9. Look more deeply into this mirror, *
     see his suffering and shameful death.

10. Consider also the endless delights, *
     the riches and honors beyond all speech.

11. Let me run without tiring
     till I come to the bridal chamber *
     and embrace you for evermore.

Psalm 138:
We Are Those Who Have Made a Covenant

Myles Coverdale (1488–1568)

1. We are those who have made a covenant with God, *
    to forsake Satan in this world.

2. We are those who have their lights burning *
    to await the coming of Christ.

3. We are those who have determined to worship God only, *
    and not the works of human hands.

4. We are those to whom Christ is precious; *
    we are those whose joy and paradise is not here.

5. We belong to another world; *
    Christ is our captain.

6. Our joy is in heaven; *
    our companions are the saints of God.

7. Why should we think it strange if troubles and adversities come upon us? *
    Can the world love you, if your hope lies elsewhere?

8. Do you expect to travel and never encounter rain? *
    Will Satan let you rest, if you will not worship him?

9. If you seek the heavenly Jerusalem where all is joy, *
    will you let yourself be delayed by storms and showers?

10. So let us like God's own children go forward apace, *
    let us hoist up our sails; the wind is at our back.

Psalm 139:
Place Your Good Spirit Within Me

Charles Wesley (1707-1788)

1. Place your good spirit within me, Lord God, *
    the Spirit of health and love and power.

2. Plant your victorious grace within me, *
    let sin never again enter my heart.

3. Cause me to walk in the way of Christ, *
    let me fulfill your law and perform your will.

4. You have said that I will keep your law *
    and I believe your word though others doubt.

5. Let me prove your word to be true *
    and enter the rest you have promised.

6. Let me forever dwell with you; *
    be my God and let me be your servant.

7. Supply my every need: *
    sustain the life you have given;

8. Fill me with the living bread,
    the manna that comes down from heaven, *
    let me hunger no more.

9. You, Lord, are holy and righteous and true; *
    remember your word of promise
    and seal me with your life-giving Spirit.

10. Open the eye of my faith, *
    overpower me with your grace.
    display your glory to me.

11. Let me gain perfection's height and fall into nothingness; *
    let me be less than nothing in your sight,
    that Christ may be all in all.

Psalm 140:
Let Our Lives Be a Song of Praise

Elisabeth Leseur (1866–1914)

1. Let our lives be first of all a perpetual song of praise; *
   let deep joy live within us.

2. Let us be like the lark that announces the dawn, *
   and awakens in every creature the love of the light.

3. Why do we put off doing the good until tomorrow? *
   Why do we wait to be wealthy before giving?

4. Is not the gift of ourselves better than money? *
   Is there ever a time when we cannot offer a tear or a smile
   to someone suffering?

5. Cannot a word from us strengthen someone in distress? *
   Cannot an act of love coming from our depths
   brighten a sad life?

6. O Light, Beauty, total love, O my God, *
   when will we love only you, you alone?

7. This burning need for justice, this loving flame within us, *
   this can only be an unconscious turning toward infinite love,
   infinite justice,
   the ultimate goodness that is God.

8. Let us despise no one, for in the worst there is the divine spark that
   can flame forth; *
   in every idea is a grain of truth to be discovered.

9. Let us not look too far ahead or too high above ourselves, *
    for in front of ourselves, right next to us,
      is often the good to be done.

10. Let us develop in ourselves divine compassion
    so as to be truly human; *
      when our inner selves expand, only God can fill them.

11. Not to accept everything but to understand everything,
    not to approve of everything but to forgive everything. *
      Not to adopt everything but to search for the grain
      of truth within.

12. There is a joy that the worst sorrows cannot destroy; *
      a light that shines in the darkest night,
      a strength that sustains us in our weakness.

Psalm 141:
Let Us Run to the Brooks of Water

Augustine of Hippo (354–430)

1. Let us run to the brooks of water, *
    let us run to the streams that give life,

2. For our God is a never-failing stream, *
    a light that will never be darkened.

3. Yet this is a light that the outward eye does not see *
    and for which our inner eye must be trained.

4. When I seek God in visible and material things, I fail; *
    when I seek God in myself, my search is unsuccessful.

5. The house of God is above me; *
    there God dwells; from there God beholds me.

6. From there God directs me and provides for me; *
    from there God calls me and leads me on to my goal.

7. In that place is a never-ending festival, *
    and the strains of music and rejoicing.

8. From that festival come the sounds that we hear inwardly, *
    though the world may be allowed to drown them out.

9. In God's presence is a celebration
    that does not begin with the sunrise, *
        nor does it end when the sun goes down.

Psalm 142:
God is the Inheritance of the Saints

Jonathan Edwards (1703–1758)

1. God is the inheritance of the saints, *
    and the portion provided for our souls.

2. God is our wealth and our treasure, *
    our food, our delight, and our dwelling place.

3. God is our ornament and diadem, *
    God is our everlasting honor and glory.

4. God is the great good who welcomes us at our death, *
    and in whom we will rise at the end of the world.

5. The Lord God is the light of the new Jerusalem *
    and the river of the water of life.

6. The beauty of God will for ever delight the saints, *
    and the love of God will be our everlasting feast.

7. The saints are blessed by the gift of God's holiness, *
    as the moon and planets are brightened by the light of the sun.

8. The saints have all their good in God, *
    and God is all our good.

Psalm 143:
Be My Will, Lord God

Douglas V. Steere (1901–1995)

1. Be my will, Lord God, *
    I open my self before you.

2. Be my will, Lord God, *
    I open my self to you.

3. You are my God, my holy one, my Love; *
    O wonderful beyond words.

4. You are the holy one, beyond all else that is; *
    I am nothing in your presence,
    yet you move me to seek you.

5. I am nothing in your presence, *
    fill me, O Holy One, with a desire for you alone.

6. Fill me, O Holy One, with a desire for you alone, *
    that you may be all in all.

7. Turn me away from self-seeking and love of possessions; *
    center my life in the desire for your love.

8. You alone do I seek, *
    in you alone is true life.

9. In pure obedience let me learn true contentment; *
    let me be nourished with the true bread of life.

10. Let me not be content with any worldly standards; *
    let me not measure my life by what others possess.

11. The life of obedience is a life of holiness; *
    there is no room for compromise or half measures:
    God must be all in all.

12. The steady peace of God is a peace at the depths of our life; *
    this abiding, enduring peace is God's gift
    to those who seek Life.

Psalm 144:
Praise God for the Sweetness

Christopher Smart (1722–1771)

1. Praise God for the sweetness of the dew on the grass, *
   and for the flickering light of the candles of prayer.

2. Praise the Creator for the speed of the horse, *
   and praise God for the lion's strength.

3. Praise God for the eagle soaring on the rising air, *
   and praise the Creator for the whale and the dolphin.

4. Praise God also for sail boats before the wind, *
   and for the green leaf in springtime.

5. Praise the all-Creator for the moon's light on new blossoms, *
   and for the swirl of stars across the night sky.

6. Praise God for men and women of prayer, *
   and give thanks for organs and choirs.

7. Praise God for amethyst, rubies, and pearls, *
   and give thanks for the widow's mite.

8. How glorious is the sun in its daily appearance, *
   glorious also is the comet and the meteor shower.

9. How glorious are the northern lights in the night sky, *
   how glorious the roar of thunder and the lightning flash.

10. More glorious still is the crown of the Savior, *
    who determined and dared and accomplished
    salvation for the human race.

Psalm 145:
No, Lord, I Will Not Feast

Gerard Manley Hopkins (1844–1889)

1. No, Lord, I will not feast on my despair, *
    nor unravel the last strands of my life,

2. Nor will I let my weariness cry out, *
    nor will I choose now not to live.

3. But why must your dark, devouring eyes still seek me out? *
    Why will you terrify me with your tempests?

4. I wake, and feel the darkness, not the day; *
    what black hours I have spent,
    how frantic to avoid your hand and flee.

5. I speak of hours but they are years, and life; *
    my lament is like dead letters sent to one now gone.

6. No greater grief is possible than mine; *
    I have been pitched past deepest pangs of pain.

7. Gall and heartburn have been my lot by God's decree; *
    I am compelled to taste the bitterness of blood.

8. Where then, O Comforter, is your promised comforting? *
    Mary, our mother, where is your relief?

9. The mind makes mountains in my path and cliffs *
    unfathomed, frightful, sheer on every side.

10. What worse enemy could I find, my Friend; *
    what worse defeat and who could thwart me more?

11. Yet death brings each life to an end, *
    and every day dies out with sleep.

12. So, too, that night of now done darkness dies *
    in which I wrestled with my God.

13. But see how new growth comes up and birds build nests again; *
    when will you, Lord of life, send my roots rain?

14. Complete your creature, dear Lord, where it fails, *
    for you are mighty, but a parent, too, and fond.

15. Meanwhile the human spirit in its bone-house, mean house, dwells, *
    the flesh-bound spirit found there at its best;

16. Immortal diamond, unencumbered, not distressed, I walk, *
    I lift up heart and eyes to glean God's glory.

17. I give God glory for the dappled things, *
    the brindled cow and stippled trout that swims,

18. For falling fruit and birds that rise through air, *
    the fallow earth and ripening fields of grain,

19. For nature, always new, renewed with each day's dawn, *
    past telling of the tongue, lightning and love;

20. Sing praise for all created things however spare and strange, *
    brought forth from God whose beauty is past change.

Psalm 146:
I Took Up a Pearl

Ephrem the Syrian (c. 306–373)

1. On a certain day I took up a pearl, *
    I saw in the pearl mysteries of the reign of God.

2. I saw in the pearl mysteries of the majesty of God; *
    it became a fountain and I drank of it mysteries of the Son.

3. I took the pearl in my hand to examine it; *
    I looked at one side but there were faces on all sides.

4. I found out that the Son was incomprehensible, *
    since He is wholly Light.

5. In the brightness of the pearl I beheld the Bright One
   who cannot be clouded, *
      and in its pureness a great mystery,
      even the Body of our Lord which is well-refined:

6. In its undividedness I saw the Truth which is undivided. *
    I saw in its purity the Church, and the Son within her.

7. I saw therein His victories and His crowns; *
    I saw His helpful and overflowing graces,
    and His hidden things with His revealed things.

8. The trumpet falters and the thunder mutters; *
    leave the things hidden, take the things revealed.

PSALM 146: I TOOK UP A PEARL

9. Like that manna which alone filled the people with its pleasure, *
    so does this pearl fill me in the place of books.

10. When I asked if there were yet other mysteries, *
    it had no mouth for me that I might hear.

11. Then I was told, "I am the daughter of the sea, the illimitable sea! *
    And in that sea is a mighty treasury of mysteries.

12. "You may search out the sea, *
    but do not search out the Lord of the sea!

13. "Have you not seen, then, the waves of the sea,
    which break the ship that struggles against them *
       while the ship that does not rebel against them is preserved?

14. "Do you then have a heart of stone *
    that you read the truth and yet run into errors?

15. "Do you not have a great fear *
    when justice is so long silent!"

16. When searching is mingled with thanksgiving, *
    which of the two will prevail?

17. When the incense of praise rises up with the fumes of disputation *
    to which of them shall we listen?

18. Prayer and prying come from one mouth, *
    to which of them shall we listen?

19. Do not be weary, my friends, *
    nor suppose that the struggle is long.

20. Death is already behind us and resurrection at hand; *
    now the light dawns and the Savior is already near.

Psalm 147:
Those Who See the Light

Irenaeus (c. 130–c. 202)

1. Those who see the light are within the light,
    and partake of its brilliancy; *
        even so, those who see God are in God,
        and receive of His splendor.

2. As God's splendor gives them life; *
        those who see God receive life.

3. The Lord our God is beyond comprehension,
    boundless and invisible, *
        yet within the capacity of those who believe.

4. For as God's greatness is past finding out, *
        so also is God's goodness beyond expression;

5. The means of life is found in fellowship with God; *
        and fellowship with God is to know God,
        and to enjoy God's goodness.

6. Men and women therefore shall see God, that they may live, *
        being made immortal by that sight.

7. God may be seen by those who bear the Spirit within them, *
        and do always wait patiently for God's coming.

8. Thus, therefore, is God revealed; *
        for God the Source is shown forth through all these operations:

9.   God is shown forth through the working of the Spirit, *
     and God is manifested in the ministering of the Son.

10. In all this God is the source and the means, *
     by which our salvation is accomplished.

11. The one who is at work in all things is God, *
     for there is one God the Source, who contains all things,
     and who grants existence to all,

12. For the glory of God is a living man or woman; *
     and the life of every woman or man consists in beholding God.

13. For the manifestation of God is made by means of the creation, *
     and affords life to all living in the earth,

14. Even more does that revelation of the Source through the Word, *
     give life to those who see God.

Psalm 148:
All the Blessings God Grants

John Wesley (1703–1791)

1. All the blessings God grants us are gifts of grace, *
    free gifts of undeserved favor;
    we have no claim to the least of his mercies.

2. Free grace formed us of the dust of the ground, *
    free grace breathed into us a living soul.

3. Free grace stamped on our souls the image of God, *
    and free grace put all things under our feet.

4. If then we who are sinful find favor with God, *
    that gift is grace upon grace!

5. Nothing we are, or have, or do,
   can deserve the least thing at God's hand. *
    whatever good may be found in us is also the gift of God.

6. Faith is no cold and lifeless assent, *
    but faith is the commitment of the heart.

7. Faith knows that only the death of Christ
   is sufficient to save us from death *
    and only the resurrection of Christ can restore us to life eternal.

8. Christian faith is an assent to the whole gospel of Christ; *
    Faith trusts in his life, his death, and his resurrection.

9. This is the salvation through faith in this present world, *
    through Christ formed in the heart.

10. Through faith your strength is made perfect even in weakness; *
    you shall prevail and march on
    until death is swallowed up in victory.

Psalm 149:
Our Faith Is Not Founded on Empty Words

Hippolytus of Rome (c. 236)

1. Our faith is not founded on empty words, *
    we are not carried away by misleading arguments.

2. We trust words spoken by the power of God, *
    spoken by the Word of God at God's command.

3. God does not seek to win us back by force, *
    but by calling us to liberty, by appealing to our free will.

4. God spoke to us first through the prophets, *
    but at last through his own dear Son.

5. His humanity was of the same clay as ours, *
    for only so could he call us to imitate his life.

6. He worked as we do, he hungered and thirsted, *
    he submitted to death and rose again to life.

7. He offered his own humanity as the first fruits of our race, *
    so we should not lose heart in suffering,
        for we too can be raised to new life.

8. We must recognize in ourselves the God who made us in God's image, *
    so we in turn will be recognized and acknowledged by our Maker.

Psalm 150:
I Rise to Live This Day

Saint Patrick (5th Century)

1. I rise to live this day *
    through the strong power of the Triune God:

2. God who is One in Three; *
    God who is Three in One;

3. Creator of the Universe: *
    on this God I call.

4. I rise to live this day, *
    by faith in the Incarnate God:

5. By faith in Christ's baptism in Jordan River, *
    by faith in his death on Calvary.

6. I stand to live this day, *
    by faith in Christ's risen life,

7. By faith in his ascent to reign, *
    by faith in his return to rule.

8. I stand before God this day, *
    through the strong love of cherubim,

9. By faith in the obedience of angels and archangels, *
    and hope to rise to Christ's right hand.

10. I stand before God this day, *
    by faith of confessors, by prayers of the patriarchs,

11. I stand before God this day, *
    by visions of prophets, by preaching of apostles,

12. I stand before God this day, *
    by virtue of the shining sun,
    and radiance of the moon by night,

13. I stand before God this day, *
    by virtue of the flashing of the lightning shaft,
    the tongues of fire, the swirling wind,

14. I stand before God this day, *
    by virtue of the stable earth, the deep salt sea,
    the ancient rock beneath my feet.

15. I rise to live this day, *
    through God's strength to uphold and lead,

16. God's wisdom to guide me, *
    God's eye to watch over me, God's ear to hear me,

17. God's word to teach me, *
    God's shield to protect me.

18. I stand before God this day *
    with the heavenly host to guard me

19. Against snares and temptations on every side, *
    against all who may wish me ill.

20. I summon today the heavenly powers, *
    to stand between me and all the hosts of evil;

21. Against each cruel and merciless enemy of my life, *
    against false teaching and idolatry.

22. I call on Christ to shield me this day *
    from all that corrupts either body or mind,

23. Wherever I travel, wherever I lodge, *
    to save me from danger in all that I do.

24. Christ be with me: before me, behind me; *
    Christ be in me: above me, beneath me;

25. Christ on my right hand and Christ on my left, *
    Christ in my resting and Christ in my rising;

26. Christ in the hearts of all those who think of me; *
    Christ in the mouths of all those who speak of me;

27. Christ in the eyes of all those who see me; *
    Christ in the ears of all those who hear me.

28. God who is One in Three; *
    God who is Three in One:

29. Creator, Redeemer, Sanctifier, *
    be my Savior this day and forever.

Bibliography

Abba Philemon, *The Essential Writings of Christian Mysticism*, edited by Bernard McGinn. New York: Random House, 2006.
Anderson, Elizabeth A., *Mechthild of Magdeburg: Selections from The Flowing Light of the Godhead*. Cambridge University Press: D. S. Brewer, 2003.
Andrewes, Lancelot, *The Devotions of Bishop Andrewes*, edited by John Henry Newman. New York: George H. Richmond & Co., 1897.
Anonymous, *The Web of Words; structural analyses of the Old English poems: Vainglory, the Wonder of Creation, the Dream of the Rood, and Judith*, translated by Bernard F. Huppé. Albany: State University of New York Press, 1970.
Anonymous, *The Theologia Germanica of Martin Luther*, translated by Bengt Hoffman. New York: Paulist, 1980.
Anselm of Canterbury, *Anselm of Canterbury: the Major Works*, edited by Brian Davies and G. R. Evans. Oxford: Oxford University Press, 1998.
Atwell, Robert (editor), *Celebrating the Saints*. Norwich: Canterbury, 1999.
Baillie, John, *A Diary of Private Prayer*. New York: Charles Scribner's Sons, 1952.
Barclay, William, *Epilogues and Prayers*. New York: Abingdon, 1963.
Barclay, William, *A Barclay Prayer Book*. London : SCM, 1990.
Baxter, Richard, *The Saints Everlasting Rest*. www.gracegems.org/book4/Baxter.htm
Benedict of Nursia, *The Rule of St. Benedict*, edited by Timothy Fry. New York: Vintage, 1998.
Bergman, Ingmar, *Four Screenplays of Ingmar Bergman*. New York: Simon and Schuster, 1960.
Bernard of Clairvaux, *Selected Works*, edited by G.R.Evans. Mahwah, N.J.: Paulist, 1987.
Boehme, Jacob, *The Signature of All Things, with Other Writings*. London: J.M. Dent & Sons, Ltd., 1912.
Brooks, Phillips, *The More Abundant Life*. New York: E.P. Dutton and Co., 1901.
Bunston, Anna, "A Great Mystery," *The Oxford Book of English Mystical Verse*, edited by D.H.S. Nicholson, and A.H.E. Lee. Oxford: Clarendon, 1927.
Bunyan, John, *Pilgrim's Progress (1678–1685)*. Virginia Beach, Virginia: CBN University, 1978.
Campbell, Roy, *Poems of St John of the Cross*. London: Harvill, 1951.
Chrysostom, John, *The Easter sermon of John Chrysostom*. http://anglicansonline.org/special/Easter/chrysostom_easter.html
The Cloud of Unknowing, translated by Evelyn Underhill. Rockport, Massachusetts: Element, 1997.

Counsell, Michael, *2000 Years of Prayer*. Harrisburg, PA: Morehouse, 1999.
Crashaw, Richard, *Poems by Richard Crashaw*, edited by A.R. Waller. Cambridge: Cambridge University Press, 1904.
Dante Alighieri, *The Divine Comedy: Paradise*, translated by Dorothy L. Sayers and Beatrice Reynolds. Harmondsworth, Middlesex, England: Penguin, 1962.
Day, Dorothy, *On Pilgrimage*. Grand Rapids, Michigan: William B. Eerdmans, 1948.
Dionysius, *The Works of Dionysius the Areopagite*, edited by John Parker. Merrick, New York: Richwood, 1976.
Dolan, John P. , "The Handbook of the Militant Christian." In *The Essential Erasmus*, New York: Signet, 1964.
Donne, John, *John Donne: Divine Poems, Sermons, Devotions, and Prayers*, edited by John Booty. New York: Paulist, 1990.
Edwards, Jonathan, "God Glorified in the Work of Redemption," in *The Sermons of Jonathan Edwards, a Reader*, edited by Wilson H. Kimnach, Kenneth P. Kimnach, and Douglas A. Sweeney. New Haven: Yale University Press, 1999.
Ephrem the Syrian, *The Pearl: Seven Hymns on the Faith*. http://www.newadvent.org/fathers/3705.htm
Evans, G. R., *Bernard of Clairvaux: Selected Works*. Mahwah, New Jersey: Paulist, 1987.
Ferris, Theodore Parker in *Give Us Grace: an Anthology of Anglican Prayer*, Christopher L. Webber, editor; Morehouse Publishing: Harrisburg, PA, 2004, p. 390.
Fry, Christopher, *Three Plays*. New York: Oxford University Press, 1961.
Hamarskjöld, Dag, *Markings*, edited by W. H. Auden and Leif Sjöberg. New York: Alfred A. Knopf, 1972.
Hambrick-Stowe, Charles E., *Early New England Meditative Poetry: Anne Bradstreet and Edward Taylor*. New York: Paulist, 1988.
Harvey, Andrew, *Teachings of the Christian Mystics*. Boston: Shambhala, 1998
Hildegard of Bingen, *Scivias*, translated by Columba Hart and Jane Bishop. New York: Paulist, 1990.
Hugh of St. Victor, *The Divine Love*. London: A.R.Mowbray, 1956.
Irenaeus, *Against the Heresies*. http://www.earlychristianwritings.com/text/irenaeus-book4.html
James, H.R., *The Consolation of Philosophy of Boethius, Translated into English Prose and Verse*. London: Elliot Stock, 1897.
John of Forde, *Sky-Blue is the Sapphire, Crimson the Rose: Stillpoint of Desire in John of Forde*, edited by Hilary Costello. Kalamazoo, Michigan: Cistercian, 2006.
Johnson, James Weldon, *God's Trombones; Seven Negro Sermons in Verse*, New York: Viking, 1927.
Jones, Absalom, *Thanksgiving Sermon, Preached January 1, 1808, in St. Thomas Church, or the African Episcopal Church, Philadelphia, on Account of the Abolition of the African Slave Trade on that day by the Congress of the United States*. Philadelphia: Fry and Kammerer, 1808.
Kierkegaard, Søren, *The Gospel of Our Sufferings*. Grand Rapids, Michigan: Eerdmans, 1964.
Law, William, *The Pocket William Law*, edited by Arthur W. Hopkinson. London: Latimer House Ltd.,1950.
Lawrence, Brother, *The Practice of the Presence of God*, Cincinnati, Ohio: Forward Movement, 1941.
L'Engle, Madeleine, *The Weather of the Heart*. Wheaton, Illinois: Harold Shaw, 1978.

Leseur, Elisabeth, *Elisabeth Leseur: Selected Writings*, edited by Janet K. Ruffing. Mahwah, New Jersey: Paulist, 2005.
Loyola, Ignatius, *Selected Prayers of Ignatius Loyola*, http://www.bc.edu/bc_org/prs/stign/prayers.html
Luther, Martin, *Paul's Epistle to the Galatians - Part First. The Battlefield. The Commander.* http://www.godrules.net/library/luther/NEWluther_d3.htm
Merton, Thomas, *What Is Contemplation?* Springfield, Illinois: Templegate, 1950.
Milner-White, Eric, *My God My Glory*. London: SPCK, 1954.
Mott, Lucretia, *Lucretia Mott: Her Complete Speeches and Sermons*, edited by Dana Greene. New York: Edward Mellen, 1980.
Nicholas of Cusa, *The Vision of God*, translated by Emma Salter. New York: Frederick Ungar, 1928.
Nicholson, D.H.S. and Lee, A. H. E., *The Oxford Book of English Mystical Verse*. Oxford: Oxford University Press, 1917.
Porete, Marguerite, *A Mirror for Simple Souls*, edited by Charles Crawford. New York: Crossroad, 1990.
Rahner, Karl, *The Practice of Faith*. New York: Crossroad, 1986.
Brother Roger of Taizé, http://www.taize.fr/en_article1510.html
Romero, Oscar, *The Violence of Love*. Maryknoll, New York: Orbis, 1988.
Rossetti, Christina, *Time Flies: a Reading Diary*. Boston: Roberts Bros., 1886.
Rowe, Elizabeth Singer, *Devout exercises of the heart, in meditation and soliloquy, prayer and praise by the late pious and ingenious Mrs. Elizabeth Rowe*. New York: Simpson & Lindsay, 1809.
Sophronius of Jerusalem, *Prayer at Daybreak*. http://www.ocf.org/OrthodoxPage/prayers/daybreak.html
Steere, Douglas V., *Testament of Devotion / by Thomas R. Kelly; with a biographical memoir by Douglas V. Steere*. New York: Harper & Row, 1941.
Taylor, Jeremy, *Rule and exercises of holy dying*. New York: D. Appleton, 1857.
Tennyson, Alfred, Lord, *The Higher Pantheism*. http://www.poetryfoundation.org/poem/174590
Teresa, Mother and Brother Roger, *Seeking the Heart of God*. San Francisco: HarperSanFrancisco, 1993.
Washington, James Melvin, *Conversations with God*. New York: HarperCollins, 1994.
Weatherhead, Leslie D., *A Private House of Prayer*. New York: Abingdon, 1958.
Weil, Simone, *Waiting for God*. New York: Capricorn Books, 1959.
Wesley, John, http://wesley.nnu.edu/john-wesley/the-sermons-of-john-wesley-1872-edition/
Wesley, Charles, *The Promise of Sanctification*. http://wesley.nnu.edu/john-wesley/the-sermons-of-john-wesley-1872-edition/sermon-40-christian-perfection/
West, Edward N., *Waiting for God*, New York: Capricorn Books, 1959.
Wilson, A.N., *John Henry Newman: Prayers, Poems, and Meditations*. New York: Crossroad, 1990.
Wright, J. Robert, *Readings from the Early Church for the Daily Office*. New York: Church Hymnal Corporation, 1991, p. 37.
Wycliffite Spirituality (14th Century), Mahwah, New Jersey: Paulist, 2013.
Yates, Miles Lowell, *Our Bounden Duty*. New York: Oxford, 1951.

Index of Authors

Abba Philemon (c. 700) Psalm 110
There is little information about Abba Philemon except that he probably lived in the seventh or eighth century in Egypt and is our earliest known source for the Jesus Prayer in the form we know it today.

Alexander, Daniel Payne (1811–1893) Psalm 38
A bishop of the African Methodist Episcopal Church, Bishop Alexander was also the founder and resident of Wilberforce University in Ohio.

Andrewes, Lancelot (1555–1626) Psalms 77, 105
A bishop of the Church of England during the reigns of Elizabeth I and James I, Bishop Andrewes chaired the committee that produced the King James Version of the Bible.

Anonymous (c. 7th Century) Psalm 90

Anonymous (14th Century) Psalm 91

Anonymous (14th Century) Psalm 111

Anselm of Canterbury (1033–1109) Psalms 98, 99
A Benedictine monk and theologian, Anselm was Archbishop of Canterbury from 1093 to 1109.

Appleton, George (1902–1993) Psalm 130
A Canadian Anglican bishop and writer who served as Archdeacon of Rangoon in Burma and later as Archbishop of Perth in Australia.

Augustine of Hippo (354–430) Psalms 12, 141
Perhaps the most significant of early Christian theologians, Augustine served also as a bishop in northern Africa.

Baillie, John (1886–1960) Psalms 82, 107
An influential twentieth century Scottish theologian and Church of Scotland minister.

Barclay, William (1907–1978) Psalms 72, 133

Professor of Divinity and Biblical Criticism at the University of Glasgow, William Barclay was also the author of a popular series of Bible studies.

Baxter, Richard (1615–1691) Psalm 69

An important seventeenth century English Puritan poet, hymn-writer, and theologian.

Benedict of Nursia (480–547) Psalm 49

Founded twelve communities for monks. His "Rule of Saint Benedict" became the most influential religious rule of life in western Christendom.

Bergman, Ingmar (1918–2007) Psalm 22

Swedish director, writer, and producer in film, theater, and television.

Bernard of Clairvaux (1090–1153) Psalms 50, 52, 80, 81

French abbot and leader in the reform of the Benedictine tradition that created the Cistercian Order.

Boehme, Jacob (1575–1624) Psalm 93

German Lutheran mystic and theologian.

Boethius (475–524) Psalm 126

Author of "The Consolation of Philosophy," an influential treatise in the Middle Ages; Boethius was a Roman senator, consul, and philosopher.

Boros, Ladislaus (1927–1981) Psalms 26, 27, 104

Twentieth century Hungarian Jesuit theologian and author.

Bradstreet, Anne (1612–1672) Psalm 1

The best known of early English poets of North America, Bradstreet was the first female writer in England's North American colonies to be published.

Brooks, Phillips (1835–1893) Psalm 51

Rector of Boston's Trinity Church and briefly Bishop of Massachusetts, Brooks is best known today as the author of the Christmas hymn, *O Little Town of Bethlehem*.

Brother Lawrence (1612–1691) Psalm 100

Served as a lay brother in the kitchen of a Carmelite monastery in Paris and is remembered for his simple guide to "The Practice of the Presence of God."

Bunston, Anna (1869–1954) Psalm 65

English poet, mystic, and novelist in the first half of the twentieth century.

INDEX OF AUTHORS   277

Bunyan, John (1678–1685) Psalm 101

English writer and Baptist preacher, Bunyan is best known as the author of the Christian allegory, *The Pilgrim's Progress*.

Catherine of Genoa (1447–1510) Psalm 33

An Italian mystic, Catherine cared especially for the sick and poor and is remembered also for her writings about her mystical experiences.

Catherine of Siena (1347–1380) Psalm 120

A woman of intense prayer and close union with God who worked for the return of the papacy from Avignon to Rome.

Chrysostom, John (347–407) Psalm 124

Archbishop of Constantinople, remembered especially for the eloquence of his preaching.

Clare of Assisi (1194–1253) Psalm 137

One of the first followers of Saint Francis of Assisi, founder of a religious order for women in the Franciscan tradition.

Clement of Alexandria (150–215) Psalm 63

One of the earliest Christian theologians and one of the first to present a philosophical analysis of the Christian faith.

The Cloud of Unknowing (14th Century) Psalm 47

An anonymous work of Christian mysticism and a guide to contemplative prayer.

Columbanus (543–615) Psalm 125

An Irish missionary who founded a number of monasteries in northern Europe in the late sixth and early seventh centuries.

Coverdale, Myles (1488–1568) Psalm 138

An English ecclesiastical reformer and preacher who produced the first complete, printed translation of the Bible into English.

Crashaw, Richard (1613–1649) Psalm 58

An English poet and teacher, one of the most important of the "metaphysical poets."

Dante (1265–1321) Psalms 48, 68

Dante Alighieri was an Italian poet of the late Middle Ages best known as author of *The Divine Comedy*.

Day, Dorothy (1897– 1980) Psalms 55, 106

An American Roman Catholic journalist and social activist.

de Caussade, Jean Pierre (1675–1751) Psalm 60

A French Jesuit priest and writer, known for his writing of "Abandonment to Divine Providence."

Donne, John (1572–1631) Psalms 2, 10, 20, 21

English priest, preacher, and poet, Dean of St. Paul's Cathedral from 1621 to 1631.

Edwards, Jonathan (1703–1758) Psalm 142

A New England revivalist preacher, philosopher, and influential Protestant theologian.

Eliot, T. S. (1888–1965) Psalm 14

One of the major poets of the twentieth century, Eliot was also an essayist, publisher, and playwright.

Ephrem the Syrian (c. 306–373) Psalm 146

A teacher of repentance, Ephrem was a Syriac Christian deacon, author of many hymns, and a theologian in the fourth century.

Erasmus, Desiderius (1466–1536) Psalms 94, 115

A Dutch Christian humanist who was perhaps the most important scholar of the northern Renaissance.

Ferris, Theodore Parker (1908–1972) Psalm 118

Rector of Trinity Church, Boston, for thirty years and one of the best known preachers of his day, Ferris was the author of several collections of sermons.

Francis of Assisi (1182- 1226) Psalm 9

An Italian preacher who abandoned wealth and security to found the Franciscan Order.

Fry, Christopher (1907–2005) Psalm 76

An English poet and playwright, best known for such verse dramas as "A Sleep of Prisoners."

Hammarskjöld, Dag (1905–1961) Psalm 67

A Swedish economist and diplomat who served as the second Secretary-General of the United Nations.

Herbert, George (1593–1633) Psalm 45

Born in Wales, Herbert was ordained a priest of the Church of England and is known for his pastoral care although he served for only three years in a country parish before his death at the age of forty.

Hilary of Poitiers (315–367) Psalm 87
Bishop of Poitiers in France and a leader in the fight against the Arian teaching about Jesus.

Hildegard of Bingen (1098–1179) Psalms 28, 43
A German Benedictine abbess, Hildegard was a writer, composer, and Christian mystic.

Hilton, Walter (1340–1396) Psalm 32
An influential English Augustinian mystic in the fourteenth century.

Hippolytus of Rome (c. 170–235) Psalm 149
Little is known about the life of Hippolytus, but his voluminous writings give us important insights into the life of the early church.

Hopkins, Gerard Manley (1844–1889) Psalm 145
A Victorian-era English Jesuit priest, author of such poems as "God's Grandeur" and "Pied Beauty."

Hugh of St. Victor (1096 -1141) Psalm 102
Author of Biblical commentaries and mystic who spent most of his life at the Abbey of St. Victor near Paris.

Ignatius of Loyola (1491–1556) Psalm 131
A Spanish Basque priest and theologian, who, with Peter Faber and Francis Xavier, founded the Society of Jesus or Jesuits and became its first Father General.

Irenaeus (c. 130-c. 202) Psalm 147
A Christian theologian of the 2nd century, he was a leader in the conflict with Gnosticism.

Jefferson, Thomas (1743–1826) Psalm 132
Diplomat, lawyer, principal author of the Declaration of Independence, and third President of the United States.

John of Forde (1140–1214) Psalms 85, 113
English priest, healer, seer, mystic, and the abbot of Forde in Dorset, England, who composed a series of sermons on the Song of Songs.

John of the Cross (1541–1592) Psalm 97
A Spanish mystic, Carmelite friar and priest who was a major figure in the Counter-Reformation.

Johnson, James Weldon (1871- 1938) Psalm 117
American author, educator, lawyer, diplomat, songwriter, civil rights activist, and author of "Lift Every Voice and Sing."

Jones, Absalom (1746–1818) Psalm 46
Jones was the first black priest in the Episcopal Church and an eloquent preacher.

Julian of Norwich (1342–1416) Psalms 6, 11, 16, 19
Julian lived most of her life as an anchorite in her parish church in Norwich, England. Her *Revelations of Divine Love* is the first book in the English language known to have been written by a woman.

Kierkegaard, Søren (1813–1855) Psalm 41
Danish theologian, poet, social critic and author, often thought of as the first existentialist philosopher.

Kelly, Thomas R. (1893–1941) Psalm 62
An American Quaker educator and mystic whose essays were first published after his death.

Kennedy, Geoffrey Studdert (1883–1929) Psalm 96
English Anglican priest and poet who served as a chaplain in World War I and gained fame for the poems he wrote out of that experience.

King, Martin Luther, Jr. (1929 – 1968) Psalm 132
An American Baptist minister and social activist who is remembered for his "I have a dream" speech in 1963.

Law, William (1686–1761) Psalms 37, 78
Priest of the Church of England whose "Serious Call to a Devout and Holy Life" is still in print today.

L'Engle, Madeleine (1918–2007) Psalm 103
An American writer whose fiction for children and young adults reflects both her Christian faith and her interest in science.

Leseur, Elisabeth (1866–1914) Psalm 109, 140
A French mystic best known for her spiritual diary and the conversion of her husband, a medical doctor and well known leader of the French anti-clerical, atheistic movement.

Lincoln, Abraham (1809–1865) Psalm 132
The 16th President of the United States, Lincoln was a statesman and lawyer who led the country through the American Civil War—its greatest political crisis.

Luther, Martin (1483–1546) Psalms 86, 127, 128
A German professor of theology, composer, priest, monk, whose writings sparked the Protestant Reformation.

Mechthild of Magdeburg (1207-c. 1290) Psalms 61, 95
A medieval mystic, whose writings described her visions of God; ignorant of Latin, she was the first mystic to write in German.

Meister Eckhart (c. 1260-c. 1327) Psalm 44
Eckhart von Hochheim OP, commonly known as Meister Eckhart, was an influential medieval German theologian and mystic.

Milner-White, Eric (1884–1963) Psalms 73, 74, 136
A decorated military chaplain, Milner-White became the founder of the Oratory of the Good Shepherd, an Anglican dispersed community.

Moody, Dwight L. (1837–1899) Psalm 119
American evangelist who conducted revival missions in England and the United States and founded the Moody Bible Institute.

Mother Teresa (1910–1997) Psalm 40
Born in Macedonia to Albanian parents, Mother Teresa founded the Missionaries of Charity, a Roman Catholic religious congregation dedicated to serving "the poorest of the poor," and spent her most important years among the poor on the streets of Calcutta.

Merton, Thomas (1915–1968) Psalm 53
American Trappist monk, widely known for his writings about spirituality.

Mott, Lucretia (1793–1880) Psalm 83
An American Quaker, Mott was a leader in the abolition movement and a prominent women's rights activist.

Nemesius of Emesa (4th Century) Psalm 5
A Christian philosopher, author of the treatise, *On the Nature of Man,* and Bishop of Emesa.

Newman, John Henry (1801–1890) Psalm 59
An English priest, theologian and poet, and convert to Roman Catholicism.

Nicholas of Cusa (1401–1464) Psalm 112
A German philosopher, theologian, jurist, experimental scientist, and astronomer who advocated the supremacy of councils over popes.

Nouwen, Henri (1932–1996) Psalm 23

A Dutch Roman Catholic priest, professor, and writer, concerned for social justice and community.

Noyes, Alfred (1880–1958) Psalm 64

An English poet, short story writer and playwright, best known for his ballad, "The Highwayman" and his lyrical verse.

Patrick of Ireland (5th Century) Psalm 150

A fifth-century Romano-British Christian missionary and bishop in Ireland; known as the "Apostle of Ireland."

Porete, Marguerite (1250–1310) Psalm 92

A French-speaking mystic and the author of *The Mirror of Simple Souls,* Porete was burned at the stake in Paris for refusing to retract her writing.

Pseudo-Dionysius (5th to 6th Century) Psalm 84

A Christian theologian of the 5th to early 6th century, who wrote a series of devotional texts using the name of a first century convert to Christianity.

Quoist, Michel (1921–1997) Psalms 34, 35, 39

A French Catholic priest, theologian and writer, Quoist is best known for his book, *Prayers of Life*.

Rahner, Karl (1904–1984) Psalm 79

Generally considered one of the most influential Roman Catholic theologians of the twentieth century, Rahner was a German Jesuit priest and theologian who taught before and after World War II at the University of Innsbruck.

Roger of Taizé (1915–2005) Psalms 24, 42, 108

The founder of the Taizé ecumenical community, Brother Roger was a Swiss Christian leader and monastic.

Rolle, Richard (1290–1349) Psalms 3, 4

An English hermit, mystic, and one of the most widely read religious writers of his time.

Romero, Oscar (1917–1980) Psalms 89, 122

Archbishop of the Roman Catholic Church in El Salvador, Romero spoke out against the poverty, social injustice, assassinations, and torture in his country until he was assassinated while celebrating Mass.

Rossetti, Christina (1830–1894) Psalm 88

One of the leading poets of the Victorian age, Rossetti wrote a variety of devotional and children's poetry.

INDEX OF AUTHORS   283

Rowe, Elizabeth (1674–1737) Psalm 57

An English poet, essayist and fiction writer who was among the most widely read eighteenth century English authors.

Smart, Christopher (1722– 1771) Psalm 144

An English poet who was imprisoned in a mental asylum for many years because of "religious mania" and for debt; his poetry received mixed reviews until the nineteenth century.

Sophronius of Jerusalem (560–638) Psalm 71

Patriarch of Jerusalem from 634 until his death, he was a monk and theologian deeply involved in the doctrinal controversies of his day.

Steere, Douglas V. (1901–1995) Psalm 143

An American Quaker, ecumenist, and author of numerous books on prayer.

Stewart, Maria W. (1803–1880) Psalm 56

An American slave who became a prominent lecturer, abolitionist, and women's rights activist.

Stowe, Harriet Beecher (1811–1896) Psalm 134

An American author who is best known for the novel, *Uncle Tom's Cabin*, in which she depicts the harsh conditions of enslaved African Americans.

Symeon the New Theologian (c. 970–1040) Psalm 31

A Byzantine Orthodox monk and poet who taught that human beings could and should have direct experience of God.

Taylor, Jeremy (1613–1667) Psalm 114

A priest of the Church of England whose book, *Holy Dying*, is one of the lasting monuments of the English language.

Teilhard de Chardin, Pierre (1881–1955) Psalms 17, 25

French idealist philosopher and Jesuit priest who was trained as a paleontologist and geologist and conceived the idea of the Omega Point: a maximum level of complexity and consciousness towards which he believed the universe was evolving.

Tennyson, Alfred (1809–1892) Psalm 70

The Poet Laureate of Great Britain and Ireland during much of Queen Victoria's reign, Lord Tennyson remains one of the most popular of British poets.

Thomas à Kempis (1380–1471) Psalms 29, 30

Author of *The Imitation of Christ*, one of the most popular guides to Christian faith and prayer.

Thompson, Francis (1859–1907) Psalm 13, 116

An English poet and mystic who spent three years on the streets of London, supporting himself with manual labor, before publishing his first poems.

Thurman, Howard (1899–1981) Psalm 18

An African-American author, theologian, and civil rights leader, profoundly influenced by Ghandi, Thurman became Dean of Howard University but left that position to found the first fully integrated, multi-cultural church in the United States in San Francisco, California.

Traherne, Thomas (1636/7–1674) Psalms 8, 15

An English poet, priest, theologian, and religious writer, little known in his own day but re-discovered in the twentieth century and hailed as a poet and mystic of major importance.

Tutu, Desmond (1931-) Psalm 135

A South African Anglican priest, archbishop, and theologian known for his work as an anti-apartheid and human rights activist; awarded the Nobel Peace Prize in 1984.

Underhill, Evelyn (1875–1941) Psalm 123

An English Anglo-Catholic writer and pacifist known for her writing on Christian mysticism.

Weatherhead, Leslie (1893–1976) Psalm 121

An English Christian theologian in the liberal Protestant tradition who was noted for his preaching ministry.

Weil, Simone (1909–1943) Psalms 7, 75

A French philosopher, mystic, and political activist attracted to Christianity but never baptized. She died of self-accepted hardship during World War II at the age of 34.

Wesley, John (1703–1791) Psalm 148

An English priest and theologian who, with his brother, Charles, and fellow priest, George Whitefield, created the Methodist movement.

Wesley, Charles (1707–1788) Psalm 139

An English priest and hymn writer who worked with his brother John to create the Methodist movement.

West, Edward N. (1909–1990) Psalm 54

Sacrist of the Cathedral of St. John the Divine, New York for many years, Officer of the Order of the British Empire and Chevalier of the Legion of Honor, and author of books on spirituality and liturgics.

Weston, M. Moran (1910–2002) Psalm 36
> Episcopal priest, social activist, and Rector of St. Philip's, Harlem, then the largest parish in the Episcopal church.

Winthrop, John (1587–1649) Psalm 132
> An English Puritan lawyer and one of the leading figures in founding the Massachusetts Bay Colony.

Wycliffe, John (1330–1384) Psalm 66
> An English scholastic philosopher, theologian, reformer, and an early translator of the Bible into English.

Yates, Miles Lowell (1890–1956) Psalm 129
> A priest of the Episcopal Church, chaplain to theological students, author, and spiritual director.

Thematic Index

Note that many texts could easily be listed under a number of headings. The following may be helpful in looking for particular subjects or themes, but it is neither definitive nor exhaustive.

Advent
Psalm 103: Listen to the Silence

Church
Psalm 133: When Your Church Awakens

Creation
Psalm 15: We Never Rightly Enjoy The World
Psalm 72: You the Creator
Psalm 114: I know That the Almighty God
Psalm 121: I Praise, Adore, and Worship

Divisions and troubles
Psalm 127: Look Down, O God
Psalm 128: God Sees Us

Easter
Psalm 12: Let Us Sing
Psalm 21: Do Not Be Strangers
Psalm 73: You Are Risen
Psalm 86: Christ Is the King of Glory
Psalm 124: Who Is There Who Truly Loves

Eucharist
Psalm 123: Come, for the Fields Are White
Psalm 125: Listen to My Voice

Faith
Psalm 42: What Matters the Most
Psalm 67: What I Ask For
Psalm 130: Lord, Increase My Faith

288   THEMATIC INDEX

Forgiveness
Psalm 57: Permit Me, O Lord

Freedom
Psalm 132: We Are to Be Like a City
Psalm 139: Place Your Good Spirit Within Me

Funerals
Psalm 20: The Angels of Heaven Have Joy

Glory of God
Psalm 48: The Glory of God
Psalm 68: Like the Sun at Noonday

God's Goodness
Psalm 6: God Has Showed Us
Psalm 11: The Whole of Creation
Psalm 60: Where Is the Secret Treasure

God's Guidance
Psalm 59: Lead Me, Light of God
Psalm 65: Strangely You Come
Psalm 70: Sun, Moon, and Stars
Psalm 105: All Glory is Yours
Psalm 136: When I Wake to a New Day

God's Love for Us
Psalm 6: God Has Showed Us
Psalm 13: I Fled from God
Psalm 18: Sometimes the Radiance of Love
Psalm 21: Do Not Be Strangers
Psalm 30: Let Our Study Always Be
Psalm 35: You Seized Me
Psalm 42: What Matters the Most
Psalm 47: The Desire for God
Psalm 48: The Glory of God
Psalm 92: You, Lord, Have Loved Me
Psalm 128: God Sees Us
Psalm 141: Let Us Run to the Brooks of Water
Psalm 142: God Is the Inheritance of the Saints
Psalm 147: Those Who See the Light

Good Friday
Psalm 90: I Was Felled to the Ground

Healing
Psalm 64: Beyond All Else

Heaven
Psalm 20: The Angels of Heaven Have Joy
Psalm 26: God Created the World

Psalm 27: Our Earthly Life
Psalm 41: The Ways of Error
Psalm 43: I Heard a Voice
Psalm 48: The Glory of God
Psalm 62: Deep Within Us
Psalm 69: How Sweet a Thought

Holy Spirit
Psalm 24: Seeking Reconciliation and Peace
Psalm 28: O Holy Fire
Psalm 61: The Holy Spirit Leads Me Gently
Psalm 74: Enter My Heart

Hope
Psalm 26: God Created the World

Jesus (Life of Christ)
Psalm 31: Come, Lord Whom My Heart Desires

Joy
Psalm 20: The Angels of Heaven Have Joy
Psalm 54: Our Desire for God

Lent
Psalm 24: Seeking Reconciliation and Peace
Psalm 27: Our Earthly Life
Psalm 29: I Will Speak to My Lord
Psalm 34: Once Again I Have Fallen
Psalm 39: Since You, Lord, Came
Psalm 45: My Life Was in Turmoil
Psalm 49: Listen Carefully to Instruction
Psalm 51: Let Us Glorify Obedience
Psalm 53: Grant Me, Lord God
Psalm 58: Lord, What Are We

Light of Christ
Psalm 31: Come, Lord Whom My Heart Desires

Love of God
Psalm 33: A Clear and Pure Love
Psalm 50: What Better Gift Could God Give
Psalm 54: Love In Human Flesh
Psalm 55: What Is It That We Seek
Psalm 64: Beyond All Else
Psalm 80: God Is Not Loved Without Reward
Psalm 85: Love Is More Precious Than Gold
Psalm 102: Tell Me, O Human Heart
Psalm 107: O Love, Beyond All Knowing
Psalm 113: Varied, Indeed, and Marvelous
Psalm 125: Listen to My Voice
Psalm 126: Why Are the Changes

Marriage
Psalm 126: Why Are the Changes

Meaning of Life
Psalm 87: When I Searched for the Meaning

Mercy
Psalm 3: Mercy Must Be on My Mind
Psalm 29: I Will Speak to My Lord
Psalm 57: Permit me, O Lord
Psalm 75: I Do Not Need Any Hope
Psalm 148: All the Blessings God Grants

Mission
Psalm 56: Paul May Plant
Psalm 123: Come, For the Fields Are White

Morning Prayer
Psalm 105: All Glory Is Yours
Psalm 134: I Turn to You
Psalm 136: When I Wake to a New Day
Psalm 150: I Rise to Live This Day

Mystery of God
Psalm 67: What I Ask For
Psalm 79: I Would Like to Be Free
Psalm 81: You Promised, Lord
Psalm 84: Now Let Us Sing the Eternal Life
Psalm 104: How Fragmentary is Human Existence

National Life
Psalm 132: We Are to Be Like a City
Psalm 140: Let Our Lives Be a Song of Praise

Obedience
Psalm 44 : True and Perfect Obedience
Psalm 51: Let Us Glorify Obedience

Offering
Psalm 2: Eternal and Gracious God

Patience
Psalm 111: Learn to Let Go of God

Peace in God
Psalm 19: So I Saw That God Is Our Peace
Psalm 89: Peace Does Not Come from Terror
Psalm 115: Peace Is the Highest Good

Pentecost
Psalm 28: O Holy Fire
Psalm 38: Descend, Lord God

Psalm 43: I Heard a Voice from Heaven
Psalm 74: Enter My Heart

Praise

Psalm 1: What God is Like Mine
Psalm 8: O Lord, Clothed With Majesty
Psalm 9: Highest, Most Powerful
Psalm 12: Let Us Sing
Psalm 14: We Praise You, O God
Psalm 63: Let Us With Pure Hearts
Psalm 144: Praise God for the Sweetness

Prayer

Psalm 37: The Greater Part of the Human Race
Psalm 66: Pure Prayer Occurs
Psalm 71: Eternal Lord and Creator
Psalm 77: Truth Beyond All Truth
Psalm 78: Consider the Treasure Within

Presence of God in all things

Psalm 114: I Know That the Almighty God
Psalm 121: I Praise, Adore, and Worship

Seeking God

Psalm 4: Let It Be Your Joy to Serve God
Psalm 6: God Has Showed Us
Psalm 7: Before All Things, God is Love
Psalm 13: I Fled from God
Psalm 17: God Spoke to Me
Psalm 21: Do Not Be Strangers
Psalm 22: I Long for God
Psalm 25: God Comes to Those
Psalm 31: Come, Lord Whom My Heart Desires
Psalm 32: What a Wonderful Change
Psalm 33: A Clear and Pure Love
Psalm 41: The Ways of Error
Psalm 42: What Matters the Most
Psalm 47: The Desire for God
Psalm 54: Our Desire for God
Psalm 76: Thousands and Thousands of Years
Psalm 91: Eternal Joy and Blessing
Psalm 95: I Have Seen a Mountain
Psalm 96: You Are the One
Psalm 97: How Well I Know
Psalm 98: Come Now, My Friends
Psalm 99: God of Justice and Truth
Psalm 101: Where, Then, Am I Called to Go
Psalm 112: My Heart Has no Rest
Psalm 120: Thanks Be to You
Psalm 129: You, O God, Are from Everlasting

Seeking God *(continued)*
Psalm 141: Let Us Run to the Brooks of Water
Psalm 146: I Took Up a Pearl

Serving God
Psalm 82: How Can I Serve You
Psalm 110: If You Would Be a Servant of God
Psalm 119: Use Me Then
Psalm 131: Take, Lord, and Receive
Psalm 137: Happy Is She Who Is Called
Psalm 138: We Are Those Who
Psalm 139: Place Your Good Spirit Within Me
Psalm 140: Let Our Lives Be a Song of Praise

Silence
Psalm 103: Listen To the Silence

Sin (confession of)
Psalm 34 : Once Again I Have Fallen
Psalm 39: Since You, Lord, Came
Psalm 88: Weigh All My Faults

Social issues (Justice and Peace)
Psalm 36: We Acknowledge, Lord God
Psalm 38: Descend, Lord God
Psalm 40: Love for the Poor
Psalm 46: In Years Gone By
Psalm 55: What Is It That We Seek
Psalm 83: Let Us Seek to Enlarge Our Souls
Psalm 86: Christ Is the King of Glory
Psalm 106: The Only Way to Express Our Love
Psalm 122: The Land Is So Beautiful
Psalm 135: Our God, My God

Suffering
Psalm 7: Before All Things, God Is Love
Psalm 109: Blessed Are You, O Lord

Thanksgiving Day
Psalm 2: Eternal and Gracious God
Psalm 132: We Are to Be Like a City

Trust in God
Psalm 16: God Speaks to Those Who Serve
Psalm 53: Grant Me, Lord God
Psalm 134: I Turn to You
Psalm 145: No, Lord, I Will Not Feast
Psalm 150: I Rise to Live This Day

Truth of God
Psalm 77: Truth Beyond All Truth

Unity
Psalm 10: We Human Beings
Psalm 17: God Spoke to Me
Psalm 91: Eternal Joy and Blessing
Psalm 132: We Are to Be Like a City

Value of Life
Psalm 5 : Consider the Dignity of Human Life

World Peace
Psalm 108: God Has Plans for a Future of Peace
Psalm 115: Peace Is the Highest Good

Worship
Psalm 117: We Come to You This Morning
Psalm 124: Who Is There Who Truly Loves

www.ingramcontent.com/pod-product-compliance
Lightning Source LLC
Chambersburg PA
CBHW070233230426
43664CB00014B/2292